The cockpit of a U.S. Air Force KC-10 refueling aircraft in flight.

Crossing

Bob Hendrickson

Crossing

© Copyright 2021, Bob Hendrickson

ISBN: 978-1-7364871-0-5, Hardback
       978-1-7364871-3-6, Paperback
       978-1-7364871-2-9, EBook – iBook

Library of Congress Control Number (LCN): 2021904295

Cover Design by Cherie Foxley

All illustrations and photographs were provided by the author from his collections or came from the public domain except where specifically noted.

Published by:
Bob Hendrickson
Stockton Springs, Maine
BobsCrossing@hotmail.com

For Spike,
Sempre e per sempre

TABLE OF CONTENTS

ACKNOWLEDGEMENTS

This has been a huge task, to capture the moving target that has been my life. Any fact that is incorrect is on me. Mischaracterizations of anyone's intentions or anything else in this book that might inadvertently offend anyone are also my responsibility. I apologize in advance. I did not mean to, so it must be the Parkinson's!

Accident investigation is a team sport. Indeed, that is one of the most important lessons I have attempted to convey in these pages. I did none of these things alone and if readers believe that, they have missed the entire point. Occasionally, I have enjoyed the support of smart, well-trained investigators. More often, I was the one playing catch-up and attempting to support them. That they remain nameless here is no reflection on their contributions. I hope I have told my story without offending any of these people, whom I so greatly admire and respect.

Without Bruce Hurd, this entire project would have been stillborn. He patiently edited my work as I hacked away at my keyboard. He gave me the encouragement I needed, demanded things of my narrative I did not know I could write, and made this all possible. Thank you, Bruce.

Not to be forgotten, I gave some pieces of the text, here and there, to many proofreaders to help me rein in my tendency toward hyperbole and get my facts straight. Thank you, Jillian, Sandy, Martha, Jeff, Tony, Aunt Helen, and all the others.

I could not have written a word if I had been dead. Thank you, Rick Packard (my old KC-135 aircraft commander) for saving my life more times and in more ways than you know.

To my family who have given me reasons to carry on through to better times ahead. Thank you, Whitney, Andrea, Kyle, and Lucas. I love you all, all the way to the moon.

And to Karen. You are my rock and my last love, ever. I lost my heart to your eyes and I am yours.

FOREWORD

By Jeff Guzzetti, FAA Supervisory Air Safety Investigator
(Retired)

I first met Bob Hendrickson long after he matured into the man he is today. He first came to my attention in the spring of 2005 as a potential recruit to be an aviation accident investigator with the National Transportation Safety Board (NTSB). As the Deputy Director for Regional Operations at the NTSB's Office of Aviation Safety, I was challenged to find experienced aviation professionals who were more than just former pilots or mechanics, to become one-person go-teams out in one of the ten NTSB regional offices. I needed people who were critical thinkers, personable, articulate, and assertive. Bob fit the bill perfectly. Unfortunately, about the time he came to my attention, he was snatched up by the FAA's elite Aircraft Accident Investigation Division (AAI-100), which provided support and expertise to the NTSB during major go-team investigations while taking care of business inside the FAA.

Fortunately, a few years later, I was able to work with Bob when I transferred over to lead AAI-100 for the last five years of my government career. But that was late in Bob's incredible life.

Until I read this book, I never knew the challenges he had experienced up to that day when he came to my attention as a potential air-safety investigator.

This book paints a vivid picture of what it's like to become an Air Force pilot, and also to excel in that capacity despite not being the "fighter pilot" Bob aspired to be. But you don't have to be in the military or a pilot to enjoy this book.

This book provides a superb treatise of the colorful and valuable life of an air-safety investigator, but you don't have to be aviation expert to enjoy this book.

This book gives an insightful and heartfelt look into the life of someone who suffers from Parkinson's Disease and its catastrophic effect on families, but you don't have to be a "Parkie" or have an interest in Parkinson's to find this book interesting and useful.

This book sheds light on what the thousands of volunteers go through – in illustrative detail – – when they give up weeks of their lives to render aid to victims of fires, catastrophic storms, and disasters – but you don't have to be interested in the world of disaster assistance to enjoy this book.

This book tells yet another story of overcoming challenges and sacrifice and heartache as a child, but you don't have to be a die-hard fan of Oliver Twist to glean meaning from it ... to enjoy it. Bob is not quite Charles Dickens, but his writing sure does approach the magnificence of Dickens' writing.

Bob's story is not fascinating because of any one of these things . . . it is fascinating because of ALL these things exist within one man's life, well spent.

Anyone who yearns to discover "Man's Search for Meaning" will find that Bob's life story is that of the "everyman" who rises to represent the best this world can offer.

When Bob asked me to write this introduction, I was blown away. I am simply not worthy, but I know Bob would disagree because he exudes humility despite his remarkable intellect and talents. Like Bob, I am now a retired air-safety investigator and spend my time writing articles and teaching about the science and methodology of aircraft accident investigations. Much of what I have learned either originated from, or was affirmed by, my interactions with Bob. I am fortunate to know him and I know you will feel the same way after you read this book.

INTRODUCTION

An unknown airliner crossing the Atlantic Ocean

"Oh God, Thy sea is so great and my boat is so small."
- Breton Fisherman's Prayer

From the time that I began flying airplanes across the great oceans of the world in November of 1980, modern jet airliners' sophistication was very much as you see it today. There were large, four-engine, jet-powered airliners like the Boeing 707 and the new 747 making the trip to Europe or the Far East almost routine. First Class Service was provided by beautiful, sophisticated, very professional flight attendants. They catered to your every need as your magic chair took you swiftly and comfortably to all the most beautiful cities in the world. All you needed to go along was the money (flying was costly) and the desire.

Much of that sophistication was a beautiful illusion, provided by the crew's teamwork and the efforts of thousands of employees who performed their "magic" out of the customers' view. The average passenger really had no way of knowing how all the moving parts came together to present such a believable illusion.

As advanced as the technology was in November of 1980, we still navigated our airplanes across the great expanses of the oceans with sextants, printed tables of star positions, slide rules, pencils, and clocks. We could only guess at weather patterns out there. Sometimes, the crew could use other navigation techniques. Still, a crossing was considered a complete success if the airplane could land on the other side of the ocean within 25 miles of the intended target!

Weather satellites were of no help to a transoceanic Airline Captain. Weather Satellites of the day were small and were usually busy taking their images of Kansas or the central U.S., or the tropics, or anyplace else but where we wanted to go because satellites were expensive and rare back then. Weathermen wanted to see pictures of clouds and rain that would significantly impact large population centers. The areas of the North Atlantic and North Pacific oceans just were not significant enough to waste such a costly resource as a weather satellite.

We did not have Inertial Navigation Systems (INS), which could navigate our airplane across an ocean simply by sensing every small airplane movement and putting that inertial information into its own internal computer to tell the pilot his position. These Inertial Navigation Systems were amazingly accurate in determining positions relative to an outside world that was utterly invisible to the black box that did the math. The early INS systems were able to keep a good idea of their position, accurate to about two miles per hour of operation without reference to the stations on the ground. When an airplane covers 400-500 miles in that hour, an accuracy of 10 miles at the other side was considered phenomenal.

We could not even reliably communicate with the outside world except with a High Frequency (HF) radio that often was impossible to use because of solar events, thunderstorms, or other things.

Indeed, we did not even have today's Global Positioning System (GPS). This satellite-based navigation system is unbelievably accurate, helping pilots to cross oceans with accuracies approaching three feet.

The pilots working in the cockpit in 1980 were essentially on their own from the time the aircraft "coasted out" (when all navigation systems and radio contact with the ground stopped receiving) until they came within range (about 100 miles) of an Air Traffic Control (ATC) Radio 6 to 10 hours later. Pointing our airplane out into a great void like the ocean required a plan, a supportive and well-coordinated crew, and a fair measure of courage.

Why courage? Because if our airplane experienced a problem halfway to Hawaii, there were no airports to drop into along the way for repairs. If we ran low on fuel because of an unexpected headwind on a flight to Europe, we could not land for more. Our chances of coasting out and never being seen again were very real.

Being the Captain on a trans-oceanic flight was no job for the timid. The Captain exercised ultimate power and was the final word on anything that took place on his (or her) ship. This was a job for a person who was decisive, smart, and well trained. The Captain in 1980 needed to be good with people, have high self-confidence, and be a great pilot.

Even today, in 2020, it is a very daunting proposition for a pilot to take his aircraft and fill it up with people, fuel, cargo, and mail until it all weighs around a million pounds. Add the expectations of the pilot's company, as well as the expectations of all 450 or so passengers and crew. Combine all that with the hopes and dreams of all the passengers and crew, their relatives, and families. And then, with all of that "baggage," taxi out to the three-mile-long runway, push up all of the throttles, accelerate that million-pound, fire-breathing metal beast filled with fuel, rubber, baggage, fire and noise, and at just the last possible moment, pull the yoke (the steering wheel) back into his lap, and take all of this insanity into the black, terrifying, unforgiving night air with the idea that "tonight, we're going to Paris!"

In the business, we call this transoceanic journey a "Crossing." As pilots, we can fly at different airspeeds and altitudes and in many types of weather. We can fly to any place the airplane has the range and capability to fly. But when we are given the responsibility to fly across an ocean, we know this is different. It takes more. It takes extra training. It takes a good crew. It takes a good plan. Most of all, it takes courage.

And so it is with each of us as we attempt to live our lives every day. There are many things in each of our lives that are routine, like mowing the grass, going to the movies, driving to the supermarket, etc. But someday, each of us will likely face our own crossing. We must cross a dangerous place or get ourselves or our family through a difficult time. If you have what it takes, the knowledge, the support from those around you, a good plan, and a fair measure of courage, you might make it. But nothing is guaranteed in this life. You also must prepare yourself for all the things that might go wrong. It takes more.

I lost count long ago of all the oceans I have crossed in my life. Some of them were real oceans, while others were events in my life that were no less dangerous just because they took place on the ground. This book is about standing on the edge, staring out into the abyss, taking a deep breath, and somehow, finding the courage to make the "Crossing."

Preparing to take off from Charles De Gaulle Airport in Paris in a TWA 767-200

PROLOGUE

The McDonnell/Douglas MD-80,
158-seat airliner in TWA livery.

The Giant Hand

As I taxied the MD-80 out to the runway, I marveled at how good it felt. After what seemed like a lifetime of working my way up the seniority ladder at Trans World Airlines, it was finally my turn, again. While I had been in the Air Force, I had been an aircraft commander (AC) and instructor pilot on one of the largest airplanes in the inventory, the KC-10 jumbo jet air refueling tanker. As the KC-10 Aircraft Commander, I was pilot-in-command of the aircraft, similar to the Captain's role on a commercial airliner. I flew that airplane all over the world, and I enjoyed the experience immensely. But then, like so many pilots in 1989, I traded in my Air Force flight suit for an airline pilot's uniform. Since then, I had forgotten how good it felt to sit in the left seat. If I could have seen a mirror, I know it would have revealed a very normal-looking man sitting in the left seat, by tradition the Captain's seat, diligently going about the arcane tasks of his profession. Here was the image of a professional, serious, and highly responsible man.

The day was one of those sunny, breezy days in early summer that families going on picnics live for. The bright sunlight glinting off the other aircraft waiting in line for takeoff was almost blinding. The grass on the infield was waving back and forth in the light breeze. The other taxiway's small dust cloud meant that the airport's mowers were out cutting the grass so there would be fewer suitable nesting sites for the ubiquitous birds.

The sky was high and clear, punctuated by little cumulus clouds which every pilot calls "bumpers." I knew they would grow with the afternoon heat to become lines of thunderstorms that the evening flights would have to contend with. But right now, the breeze was out of the northwest, right down Runway 30 and the temperature was in the mid 70's. Our aircraft's takeoff performance would be unaffected by the heat that would come later in the day.

"What a gorgeous day!" I said aloud, to no one in particular. "Makes you want to take up flying."

"Yeah," said the First Officer. "That's what all these other guys are thinking. What a mess."

This was the mid-morning rush to get out of St. Louis, and we were just one of the many airplanes waiting in line for our turn to takeoff. The plane rocked gently back and forth in the turbulent exhaust of the Boeing 757 in front of us.

As I looked out through the windshield's thick glass, an American Airlines 737 touched down on the runway. The little puff of smoke from the tires and the low rumble of the thrust reversers as he faded away off to my left said very little about the sublime balancing act the pilot had just performed, bringing down his 100,000-pound airplane in such a way that the passengers in back hardly even looked up from their magazines.

"Nice," I mumbled.

In the cockpit, a different set of noises was demanding my attention. The engines' distant whine, the little whooshing noise of the cooling fans, the chatter on the radios, and the "WHOOP WHOOP - PULL UP!" command from the overhead speaker as the First Officer tested his Ground Proximity Warning System.

"Okay, I am ready. You want the before takeoff?

I nodded. "Yes, please."

"Okay. BEFORE TAKEOFF CHECKLIST," he read. "Flaps and runway."

"Ahh, Flaps 15, green light, Runway 30 Right at St. Louis."

"Flaps 15, green light, 30 Right at St. Louis," he confirmed. "Takeoff Data and Airspeed Bugs."

"125, 135, 145, 2.45 EPR, bugs are set," I replied.

"That checks. Engine Anti-Ice?"

He continued to read the checklist, and I re-confirmed all the critical readings in the cockpit, all our other settings, and every measurement to be sure that we were ready to go and hadn't forgotten anything. Finally, he said "Down to the line."

"Okay," I responded. "We'll hold it there till we're cleared to go."

Once again, I marveled at how good it felt to be Captain of my own MD-80. As airliners go, it was a small one, unless you count the short-haul commuter airplanes, the small aircraft which were usually distinguished by their propellers and their poorly deserved nickname of "Weed Eaters." Those airplanes with propellers instead of jet engines can be much more complex to fly. I know many of the pilots in those smaller planes are just as talented as our TWA MD-80 pilots. Some, maybe even more so, but timing is out of our control, and so is luck in the airline business. That pilot flew a "Weed Eater," while I was flying my MD-80. I could not have been happier.

"T-W-A 495, taxi into position and hold," the radio squawked.

"That's us," I said, pushing up the throttles. "Below the line items."

"Roger tower, T-W-A 495 is on to hold," the First Officer radioed back. I heard him pick up the Public Address (PA) microphone and say: "Ladies and Gentlemen, we have been cleared onto the runway for our departure. Flight Attendants, please be seated for takeoff." Then, after hanging up the PA, he continued. "Below the line items. Clear right, squawking .... "

I pushed up the throttles slightly to taxi us "on to hold" – lined up on the runway with engines in idle power, waiting for clearance to takeoff.

Driving an MD-80 into takeoff position on the runway is quite different from putting a SUV into a tight parking spot at the mall. For one thing, the pilot is sitting way out in front of the machine, and the object is to get the center of the plane onto the centerline of the runway with as little wasted space behind the aircraft as possible. Every pilot knows the three useless things in aviation: the altitude above you, the fuel you have burned, and the runway behind you. This is the lesson all pilot-trainees get drummed into them again and again. "Don't be concerned with what is in the past. You are going to be busy enough dealing with what is coming next."

So, I taxied straight out onto the runway and went forward until my seat was almost to the far side of the pavement. This put my main gear just short of the centerline. I pushed in a little asymmetric power and started the hard-left turn to bring the nose around, and just like that, we were on the centerline. I eased the power levers to idle and applied gentle pressure on the toe brakes, and we were in position and ready to go.

"Trans World 495, traffic is on a three-mile final. Turn right after takeoff heading 090. Wind 300 at 5. Cleared for takeoff."

"T-W-A 495, heading 090, cleared for takeoff," the First Officer repeated the clearance.

"Okay," I said. "Ready? Here we go."

We were cleared for takeoff. Once again, I allowed myself just a quick pause to marvel at how satisfying this was. This is the moment in every flight when the machine comes alive. No longer is it an oddly shaped bus with unfortunate appendages I have to be very careful of as I maneuver around the crowded parking ramp using a little steering wheel the size of a salad plate down by my left knee. No longer must I squeeze between parked airplanes, ground equipment, buildings, jetways, and other obstacles. Takeoff is the time when the aircraft enters its element. Now it becomes just me, us, the machine, and the beckoning sky.

I could feel the airplane's acceleration as it began to push into the small of my back. I felt as if a beautiful, invisible force was pulling me and my machine forward and up. God, it felt so alive. It felt so good!

"Set power," I directed the First Officer.

"Rog ... 80 knots ... Vee One ... Rotate."

"Okay," I thought. *"A little back pressure on the yoke and the nose comes up just like that."*

That's when the bell started ringing.

"Engine Failure!"

It was the First Officer.

"What?" I asked. "Engine Failure?"

But even as I asked, I could see the nose beginning to drift off to the left.

"No sweat. I've done this a million times (in the simulator). Just a moderate push on the right rudder to keep the nose tracking straight and adjust the pitch to hold the airspeed. Just another V1 cut. We do these all the time."

"Watch your airspeed!" he yelled.

"Yeah, well, the nose is a little high, but we're barely climbing as it is!

"What's the matter with the wings?"

My controls were like mush. I couldn't seem to keep the wings level.

"Would you shut off that damned bell!" I yelled at the First Officer.

"You're descending!" He yelled back. "Oh, God! Climb, climb!"

"Oh shit," I said to myself. *"This damned thing is rolling over on its back and I've got all the rudder and aileron in that I can.*

"Nothing is working! Fly you old crate!

"What's wrong with this thing?

"Shit!"

I felt as if some giant hand had taken control of the airplane and pushed it. Looking out the window, I could see the horizon was already at 90 degrees (meaning that the airplane was rolling over and the wings were perpendicular to the ground), and the trees were getting larger fast. The rational part of my brain was telling me there was only about one second to impact, and nothing I could do was going to change the ballistic course we all were following. The survival instinct, though, kept my hands and feet on the controls, pushing and praying that something would have some kind of effect. A UPS delivery truck flashed by the window, and it was way too large.

I remembered hearing somewhere that the most common last word spoken on crash tapes was the word "shit."

As the trees grew in the windscreen, sure enough, I could hear the First Officer sitting in his seat, saying "shit, shit, shit."

"So this is what it's like," I thought. No real fear, just an overwhelming sense of sadness. I always thought I would have more time.

"I wonder why it happened today?"

Once again, I heard the bell ringing. Somehow, a last vestige of pilot training expressed itself, and I let go of the yoke, reached up to the glare shield, and silenced the damned bell.

I woke up to the staccato ringing of the telephone. I was completely disoriented. It was absolutely pitch black wherever I was, and I didn't even know which way to roll in my sweat-soaked sheets to get to the phone's insistent ringing. All I could do was feel my way around my immediate surroundings like a blind man trying to figure out where I was.

My flailing hands came in contact with the headboard. It was some kind of wood or something, so I knew right off I wasn't at home. I don't have a headboard on my bed.

The phone rang again. It stopped. It rang again. I did know that it was near my head and off to the right somewhere.

After a few more moments fumbling around in the dark, I found the thing and picked it up.

"Hello?"

"Mr. Hendrickson? Geoff at the Front Desk with your wakeup call. It is 4:30, sir."

"Okay. Thanks," I responded, disoriented by my middle of the night wake-up call.

"*Oh yeah.*"

It came to me in newsreel flashes and bits and pieces of body parts as I started to remember.

"*This is Oklahoma City. The Cessna Citation. Five dead. I need to get up. I am not the Investigator in Charge of this one. That would be Kris. Easier in some ways. More challenging in other ways. It is Day Two, and it is supposed to be snowing outside. That would make it colder at the crash scene, but it would not smell so bad.*"

I hung up and started fumbling for the light switch. Pickup in one hour - - another day in the glamorous life of an aircraft accident investigator.

As I rolled my feet out of bed and onto the cold wooden floor, I wondered, for the millionth time, if I really was in control of my life, or like the MD-80 pilot in my dreams, some "Giant Hand" was pushing me around? Had I made the decisions that had led me here, or was I just "along for the ride?"

1

CONSTELLATIONS

The Lockheed Constellation over New York

"The air is an extremely dangerous, jealous, and exacting mistress. Once under the spell, most lovers are faithful to the end, which is not always old age."

– Sir Winston Churchill

I grew up in Houston, Texas, home to NASA and all the astronauts. To say that I wanted to be like them, fly in space, and go to the Moon, would be the understatement of the century. Much like every other young boy of the 1960s,

I was enamored with all things space. I positively geeked out about all of it, even before the term "geek" gained popularity.

It began while I was playing in my backyard. The roar of mighty engines would draw my attention to the sky, where I was privileged to see a magical apparition flying right over my house coming into Houston's small airport. It might be a Lockheed Constellation, a DC-3, a DC-6, or maybe a C-119, all coming from places I could only dream about. I dreamed of high adventure and heroic deeds done, and my wanderlust grew within me, bounded only by my imagination.

When NASA began its historic exploits in Houston, I was just a few miles away from the Houston Space Flight Center, the main base for the astronauts and all their machines. Back at my home, all I could do was dream and practice in anticipation of the day when I could ride the rocket. I would sit in a confined space (under my bed), pretending to communicate with Mission Control on my walkie-talkie, as I practiced powered descents to the surface of, well, any-place but the Earth. I built all the Revell and Aurora models, hundreds of them: airplanes, aircraft carriers, tanks, sailing ships, and all of the U.S. space ships – – Mercury, Gemini, Apollo, and later, the Shuttle. They hung from my ceiling and stood on just about any flat surface in my crowded room.

I did not comprehend what it meant to fly one of these aircraft in wartime. It did not occur to me, except as an academic exercise, that I could be shot at and killed just for standing close to one of these machines in a war. I never had a passing notion that these were weapons and that I needed to come to grips with that aspect if I had any hope of a realistic chance of achieving what I was interested in. I just wanted to go fast, fly upside down, and "ride the rocket" like my astronaut heroes: Alan Shepard, Gus Grissom, John Glenn, Scott Carpenter, Wally Schirra, Gordon Cooper, Deke Slayton, and all of the heroes that followed ... that was my secret dream.

I suppose the difference, in my case, was that I did not just play at being an astronaut. I studied it. I was a voracious reader. I read all that I could from the current crop of science fiction writers that I could find. Between Isaac Asimov (who was the first to develop the three laws of robotics), Robert Heinlein (who wrote about lots of political utopias and dystopias), Poul Anderson, Ray Bradbury, and Arthur C. Clarke (who introduced the first, practical notion of the communication satellite) my imagination knew no limits. These authors described things that had not yet happened and portrayed how these things would affect the humans in their stories. In doing so, they illuminated the path of less imaginative people (like me) who came later and made many of their ideas real.

I also followed the realities that were taking place at NASA by finding and reading everything I could on aviation, rocketry, human factors, and anything "space" or "science." I wandered through the stacks in the Houston Public Library. I read trade journals and college monthly magazines like *Sea Secrets* (published by The University of Miami) because biology counted, too. I always wanted to know why and how. As a result of my curiosity, I was introduced to things like the physiological, physical, and psychosocial effects of long-term isolation.

I quickly grasped the basic concepts of orbital mechanics, even though a better understanding of these laws was still an emerging science at the time. I could discuss things like the somatogravic illusion, startle effect, abnormal physiological factors, visual illusions, and crew resource management, even before some of these things had names. I learned the difference between hypemic hypoxia and histotoxic hypoxia and how that affected the time of useful consciousness in healthy humans. The list was endless, it seemed. These were concepts that were not yet important to me, but they would be, someday.

Yes, I was a geek, but my friends just called me "Smarty Pants." My Mom and Dad thought there was something special going on with their youngest son (me), so they asked a neighbor, who happened to be studying to be a clinical psychologist, to give me a test to see what was going on. He administered the standard IQ tests to me. I thought the pictures and games were fun! Apparently, he was suitably impressed because all my father ever told me of the results was that the neighbor did not know how to score some test sections. I had scored so high, my results were off the scale. Our neighbor did not realize scores above 180 on the IQ test were even possible, so I genuinely do not know what my actual score was. I only knew it was really, really high.

As a result, instead of starting me out in kindergarten like everyone else my age, my parents put me in first grade. After they saw that I did not do well. being the youngest kid in the class, they resisted the school system's repeated efforts to move me up more quickly. I never did ask my parents why they resisted letting me go at my own pace, but I believe they knew I did not possess the emotional maturity. In retrospect, they were right. I was barely mature enough for the path I was on. My grades in class conduct proved that point – they were very marginal every place I was ever scored on that measure.

So, with a tested IQ in the top 0.5% of the population, my father was happy to tell all his friends he had a certified Mensa in his home (Mensa is an international society of those individuals who have an IQ in the top 2% of the population). From then on, my family just sat back and watched me go. They believed I would be okay simply because of my high intelligence, and, as a result, they spent more of their time concerning themselves with the very real and immediate needs of my brother. That was a decision that had consequences far beyond those years.

I knew I was a gifted child. But, more to the point, I believed that I had not *earned* my blessing in any way. I knew my gift was mine by an accident of birth. Since it was a gift, it seemed only right I should share it with others. I just did not know how. It was as if I had been given a pocketful of money I did not earn. I felt I should keep enough to live on and do something else with the remainder. Something noble. To do anything else would be selfish. I knew that whatever I did with my "gift," it needed to be _worthy._

While I know many people would have gladly traded places with me, I felt these extraordinarily high expectations were, in some ways, a great burden. This feeling dogged every decision I made for much of my youth.

My family tree was filled with great mentors, however. I knew no wiser men than my grandfather, my Uncle Steven, and my father – they were my Three Wise Men. I was lucky enough to sit on the living-room floor, listening intently while they had lively discussions on the topics of the day like global geopolitics, population control, evolution, religion, and abortion, just to name a few. My father always admonished me to speak from knowledge and not emotion. To speak from an educated perspective using facts, and not from unsubstantiated "beliefs" and hyperbole. The truth is, I learned so very much by just sitting and listening to them. They were terrific. Their deep understanding of how things worked and how those things were affected by and affected other things around them was evident whenever they spoke. I grew up believing that they had all the answers. Of course, as I grew up, I learned they did not. Nevertheless, I have been in awe of these three men all my life.

William (Billy) and Kathryn Loretta (Retta) in August 1947

My mother, the former Kathryn Loretta Hough (Retta), was 16 when she met a young man of 18 named William LeRoy Hendrickson (Bill). They were popular in high school and had a love affair, which was hot enough to melt camera lenses many years later. That they were very much in love was evident, not just from the pictures, but also because their love lasted a lifetime. They were married on November 25, 1949 when he was 20 and she was 18. My big brother Danny was born (as the joke went) nine months and twenty minutes after the ceremony, on September 2, 1950. I was the Bobby-come-lately three years after that on September 29, 1953. Although I can vouch for the fact that their life was not easy, I greatly respected that their marriage was as healthy at their passing as any I have ever known.

It was clear to me, having watched them, that they had to work hard at it every day. Marriage is not easy. What can be easy is complacency. Somehow, despite their youth, they knew this. I was lucky enough to see their commitment to one another in action right up to the hour of my father's passing on June 21, 1990, at the age of 60 -.

My father died from a disease that was saddled with misunderstanding and social stigma in 1990. He and my mother felt it best to keep its true origin from everyone except their sons and one or two family members lest they both be stigmatized and misunderstood as well. My father died from Acquired Immunodeficiency Syndrome (AIDS). As I stood at his bedside at his death and watched him struggle just to breathe, I wondered how my big, strong father had come to this.

Karposi's Sarcoma is just one of the many ways AIDS can kill you. It is a horrible way to die. My father was gasping for air and suffocating right up to his final breath. I stood by his bed and said good-bye. Because he could not speak, I did most of the talking. He knew and I knew this would be our final fairwell. To the very last minute, however, he thought of his family. When he had said his good-byes to me and my wife Karen, who was by my side, he sent us across the street to retrieve an order from his doctor. While we were running this 10-minute errand, he passed away. I don't know how he did it, but it clearly was the merciful thing to do at that point.

The Houston Police Department has the report. I know that he was never unfaithful to my mother and I have wished I could have gotten my hands on the two men who gave him that awful disease. The police said he had been attacked while inspecting a construction site as a part of his job. Well, they died before he did, and they died in jail, so I hope they received their justice somewhere. To this day, I have not talked with all of my family about any of this. A few of them know, but much of the stigma attached to that disease remains, so I let that sleeping dog lie.

My mother passed on in 2009. She went into the hospital for a routine cardiac stent procedure on July 23rd of that year. Due to a medical error by the surgeon, she never came out. As soon as I heard that something had gone terribly wrong with a procedure that was supposedly a minor surgery, I flew to Houston. I asked the nurse, how this could happen? This was supposed to be ROUTINE!

Well, she said, the cardio-vascular surgeon decided, at the last minute, to change from inserting a stent in one of her coronary arteries to putting one in her neck, and he went ahead and placed it in my mother without any further testing. The stent failed hours after she came out of the surgery. I had spoken to her after the procedure and she felt great. Sometime after I hung up, the stent failed and sent pieces through her arteries and into her brain. At that point, there was nothing they could do.

So, standing alongside my brother and his family, we removed life support from the woman whose love and generosity had brought my brother and me into this world. We stood there helplessly as she died.

I never really could go after the surgeon. He used his best judgment, and he made what turned out to be a fatal mistake. I knew with great clarity how hard it is to play you-bet-your-life with someone else's life. I did it every time I got to Vee One (the speed where the pilot makes the decision to continue the takeoff or stop the aircraft on the runway) with a load of passengers. I was not sure enough that the circumstances I described were absolutely correct – that I understood them completely. Indeed, I was not sure enough to end the career of a cardio-vascular surgeon who, the last time I saw him, was sitting in his car crying. At the end of the day, I could do nothing to bring my mother back, so I sent this dog to lie down and sleep with the other one.

I always envied them the affection and grace with which my mom and my dad treated one another. I know that somewhere, they are in one another's arms, like that day back in August of 1947 when that picture of them was taken and foretold their lifelong future.

Well before those terrible events, though, I was trying to deal with being a three-year-old little brother. As the younger of two boys, I idolized my big brother. I thought the sun rose and set with him. He taught me my numbers before I could walk, and I shared his love of learning. But nature or genetics had played a cruel trick on him. My loving, smart big brother was born with a disease called congenital glaucoma. He was born with perfectly normal sight, but his eyes were missing an important piece.

The eye is filled with a gelatinous substance called the vitreous humor. In an average, healthy person, this vitreous humor is filtered through a microscopic canal that takes the old or decaying vitreous humor away and filters it, much like a kidney would filter the blood. The eye replaces that which was removed. My brother was born without these canals. Not only was there no removal of the old vitreous humor, the new vitreous humor created from the fluid's normal flow within the eye caused the internal pressure of the eye to increase. This is a condition known as glaucoma.

The doctors tried to relieve the pressure in his eyes by periodically using a hypodermic needle to remove some of the fluid. This was a particularly brutal solution to my brother's problem, and I spent hundreds of hours at his bedside in the hospital, wishing he did not have to go through it and wishing I were anywhere else.

My big brother underwent this procedure, and others like it, hundreds of times. From the age of six to sixteen, the doctors and my brother fought an epic battle for his sight. Eventually, his eyes died as a result of the complications from so much surgical trauma. Soon, his eyes were replaced by two glass prosthetic eyes.

His illness was terrible in so many ways. The result was awful for him. He lost his sight while he was still very young. He knew what a sunset looked like, yet he also knew that he would never see one again. There were so many things that were simply lost inside him. As his younger brother, I remember thinking what a great tragedy it was for him.

I remember watching him from across the room and trying to imagine what that kind of loss must be like, but I could not conjure the feeling up in my head. It was simply unthinkable. It also drove us apart as a family. My parents loved my brother, and I believe they felt a certain amount of guilt for his blindness. I have no idea why they would feel this way. They were utterly blameless, as far as I knew.

Still, due to this guilt, they tried, on their limited income, to provide him with everything he needed or wanted. My mom and dad bought him record players, guitars, trips to camp, toys, and clothes. They paid for his college, and later, they bought him a home and made sure he never owed the bank a single dollar. My parents were joined by other family members like grandparents, aunts, and uncles in this shower of gifts. My family, both nuclear and extended, was stretched to the breaking point. Yet, they continued in this way for years, and ironically, through it all, their self-imposed guilt remained.

The Hendricksons at Easter, 1955
Parents - Bill and Retta / Boys - Danny and Bobby /
and grandmother's cocker spaniel, Blondie.

As his little brother, I resented the attention he received. With the benefit of a bit of age and distance, I feel terribly guilty about my reaction to all of this. I wanted a record player, too. I wanted a guitar. I wanted the other things, but my family had other plans for me. I was supposed to be my brother's caregiver. It was my job to take him places, read to him, clean up after him when necessary, help with his homework, drive him on dates, and to be there, beside his hospital bed, holding the catch basin for his puke when he emerged from another of his seemingly endless string of eye operations.

As soon as I was old enough, I fulfilled these obligations for my brother, but I did not do them gladly. I was jealous. I felt penned in. Most of all, I felt my family had, unknowingly, handicapped him even further by doing things for him he should have been doing himself, and this made me furious because I loved him. I saw his abilities and potential dying within him. I yearned desperately to be free of my parents, him, his situation, and most of all, his disease.

The contrast between Danny and me must have been very acute for my father. Whenever I expressed my frustrations to him, he always had the same reply: "You are fully capable. After you have read his lessons to him, go get a job!"

And so I did.

The variety of jobs I worked at was mind-boggling. I was a tire changer at a Goodyear Store. Besides actually changing tires, I did re-possessions of appliances for them ... in Houston, Texas! I sold men's clothing at a men's store named Ben's. I worked common labor on some of Houston's high-rise buildings. I sold hot dogs at Der Wienerschnitzel. I mowed miles and miles of lawns. I was an auto mechanic. I ran a pool hall. I sold advertising for "James' All Art Signs." I was an apprentice electrician. I was a carpenter. I sold fireworks for a couple of seasons. I was in several bands with my guitar. I volunteered at the Houston, Texas Lighthouse for the Blind making books, and I even worked as a shooter's helper, loading holes in the ground with dynamite for a geophysical field crew looking for oil in Nevada.

With the money I earned, I bought that guitar. I bought a bicycle. Sometimes I bought a toy or maybe a model airplane that caught my eye. When I was 16 years old and got my driver's license, I even bought a 1962 Volkswagen for $400 that I had to push start all over Houston.

I certainly learned how to work and hold a job, but I really learned that all the money I saved could not buy the attention my parents continued to give to my brother. Despite everything I did (both bad and good), I could not get their recognition. I left home in 1971, looking for something that was missing. I have spent my life since then, searching for love and affection that has never been able to fill the void within me.

2

KIP

Janette Ann Hurley

"Her ways were free, and it seemed to me,
That the sunshine walked beside her."

– Tecumseh Valley (Lyrics) by Townes Van Zandt

She had what I thought was a strange nickname. "Kip." Her real name was Janette. Janette Ann. But she preferred Kip, and so it was.

She was absolutely the most beautiful girl I had ever seen. We were each 14 years old; she was a bit older. Her hair was almost blonde, and it was as straight as it could be

13

as it fell on her shoulders; perfect yet unkempt. Her deep, brown eyes always seemed to twinkle, even when she was trying to be serious. She was self-assured and confident as we sat on the school bus going to the Texas Gulf Sulphur plant, somewhere in south Texas. She sat about six feet from me, laughing and enjoying the ride with another pre-high school girl who was completely invisible to me. I sat one row back and on the other side of the aisle, alone, which was as close as I dared. I was a nerd. I knew it, I accepted it, and I lived with it, but <u>Oh My God!</u> I felt like I had been skewered and stuck to my seat. I could not have looked away from her if I had tried.

This was the Spring Branch School District's 1967 version of the "Summer Science Program." In a way, it was summer camp, and STEM (Science, Technical, Engineering and Mathematics), and babysitting all together. It was offered to our parents as a way to give their busy, precocious children something to do during the long, hot, Texas summer with the added plus that they might learn something. Idle hands are the Devil's tools, after all.

The Summer Science Program had plenty of classroom experiences for us at the school district's Science Center, but the most popular days for all of us were the field trips. In 1967, we were more innocent, and we enjoyed getting out and exploring our world. The field trips took us to museums, wildlife preserves, geological explorations, NASA (of course!), and to production facilities like the Texas Gulf Sulphur plant to see how they mined sulphur.

Actually, we found out there are a number of ways that companies mine sulphur. Mostly, it is dug from the ground by either conventional mining or strip-mining techniques. However, these mining techniques leave terrible scars on the earth. In 1967, Texas Gulf Sulphur used the Frasch extraction method in which steam is pumped into the earth and melts the sulphur so it can be pumped to the surface. It sounds like it is: hot, stinky, and complex, and it is!

All I remember of the plant was the smell of brimstone, the heat of the steam they used to melt the yellow stuff so they could pump it out of the ground, and the loud cacophony of the huge pumps. All in all, it was a fine show, but I saw only Kip. Even today, more than 50 years later, I do not know how I enticed her to share my bench at the lunch break, but she did.

Kip was sophisticated and, I thought, worldly for a 14-year-old girl. She was very bright, witty, and I learned that she played a guitar and sang in the school choir, just like me. The idea of learning songs on our guitars and singing in a popular music group was exciting for both of us. We would both be in the "Young Sounds" when we got to high school in just a few weeks. It just got better and better!

Our lunch that day was over way too soon. As we picked up our brown paper bags and tossed them in the barrels, I did not know how I was going to keep her near me. *"She must have a boyfriend,"* I thought. Oh well, I was used to being forgotten, so I was prepared. *"That's okay. I will never forget this day, anyway. I had lunch with the prettiest angel in the class."*

When the tour was over, we all went to the school bus for the hours-long ride home. Kip sat beside me as if it were the most natural thing in the world. Wow! We talked about everything and nothing and had a great time learning that we had so much in common and that we shared so many of the same dreams. Soon, she looked me in the eyes, reached out and took my hand – my hand! – in hers. Then she tucked herself up under my arm and I held her tight.

We either sat that way for an instant or for the rest of my life, I really am not sure. But I do know that the world stopped for at least 30 minutes. I stopped breathing for an hour or so because I didn't want to scare her off. We looked out the windows at the flat plains of the Gulf Coast and talked some more about everything and nothing. We continued our long nothing conversation as the noisy school bus roared on through the hot, Texas night. When she put her head on my shoulder and I smelled her soft perfume for the first time, the smell of brimstone was forever banished from my thoughts and I don't remember a single thing (other than her) until the night the house burned down.

3

BURNING HOUSES

For the next two years, Kip and I were inseparable. The years between 14 and 16 are so full of learning, and growing, and becoming adults for everyone that age. We were no different. We had each other between 1967 and 1969 when we went through those most innocent of ages of 14, 15 and 16. In the history of the United States and, indeed the world, it would be difficult to use a term like "innocent" to describe those days where our fractured country was deeply divided because of the Vietnam War, political assassinations, and racial injustice.

Despite those turbulent times, Kip and I were one, a unit – we were together, and we had each other. We were able to slide through those crazy years and still know that we had something special. We had both quit looking. At least in that, we were set.

February of 1969 was unusually warm in Houston. NASA had just flown Apollo 8 around the moon, and the eventual landing of Apollo 11 was coming soon. Kip and I had just recorded a demo of a song she had written. She was working on landing a recording contract, and I was happy to help wherever I could. The Beatles had just released "The White Album." Led Zeppelin had just released their first album. Kip had a copy of the Beatles, and I had brought along a new artist I had heard of named Townes Van Zandt. We met at her house to swim in her pool and listen to our new vinyl records.

In much the same way that I was a nerd for STEM things, Kip was kind of a nerd for musical things. When she said that she wanted to "listen to" a new album, it was not what most people think. One of us would buy the album, and we would spend hours and hours of picking up the needle and putting it back down again to get that specific phrase, or to memorize a particularly nice riff, or just to let the artists' emotion wash over us. That was how we "listened to" some of the greats – from the Beatles and Led Zeppelin to Jelly Roll Morton, Lead Belly, Sinatra, Opera, Broadway, Joni Mitchell, Johnny Cash, and everything in between. To say that our tastes were eclectic would have been a huge understatement.

On this one special evening, we were "listening" to something, but it had been a long session and it was late.

"Wow," I said. "How did it get to be so late? What is this, Friday?"

"Um, Yes. Friday. You don't have to be anywhere tomorrow, do you?"

"No, I'm off." I thought for a minute. "But I suppose I will have to go home soon." I paused and thought some more. "Do you remember that line from the Beach Boys song, 'wouldn't it be nice if we were older?'"

"Then we wouldn't have to wait so long?" she asked dreamily.

"Yeah," I continued. "Only I really like the part that goes 'we could say good-night and stay together.'"

Kip looked at me, quizzically. Then, without another word, she reached over and kissed me. "I love you so much."

"Oh, God. Me, too," I stammered back.

Her hands were a bit tentative, but her lips met mine and I melted into putty. She pulled the string on the front of my swimsuit and slowly reached inside. What she found there electrified me, and she was smiling to see me squirm. I fumbled with her clothing. She just smiled and stopped me and pulled up her dress.

"This will be easier," she whispered.

There is a first time for everything, and this was the first time for Kip and for me. We were both clumsy, I suppose, but I did not see anything except the beauty of her body and the smile on her face. Our inexperience simply did not matter to either of us. We did great! I only remember an indescribable feeling that I was exactly where I belonged, and I wanted it to go on forever.

As these things go, I suppose it was over pretty quickly.

In the afterglow, I was contemplating the warmth and shape of her perfect body when she turned her face to mine and asked, "Did you finish?"

"What? Of course, I did. It was wonderful. What do you mean?" I asked.

"Uh, well, did you get out of the house before the fire started?"

My heart sank.

"*Aw shit*," I thought. "*Was I supposed to pull out? I didn't even think about it! Argggggh!*"

"Uh, no. Was I supposed to?"

"Well, yeah, I suppose." She lay back and smiled at the ceiling. "That's okay. First time's never the charm! We just need to be more careful in the future! Did you like it?"

"Oh, Kip. You know it. I just hope you're right about, well, you know."

"Not to worry," she said. And we drifted off to sleep.

That night, we did as the Beach Boys had dreamed of.in their song when we said good-night and stayed together.

There is a first time for everything ... and a last. This, tragically, was both.

At four weeks, she missed her period.

At six weeks, she went to the doctor (no such thing as Early Pregnancy Tests in 1969) and the rabbit died, appropriately.

Kip was pregnant.

"SHE'S WHAT?" My mom and dad looked at each other and back at me.

"Jesus H. Christ! What are you going to do now? You're SIXTEEN!"

"We're going to get married and keep the kid," was my response as I felt Kip squeezing my hand.

In the lead-up to this meeting with my parents, Kip and I had six weeks to think about it. While we dreaded telling either set of parents, we both felt that we stood a better chance of convincing my parents to trust us and give us their blessings to do what we wanted: get married and keep the kid. So, there we were, standing in front of them and pleading our case.

I felt that I could see our path forward; finish high school, get a job, and grow our little family. It was happening pretty fast – much faster than we had wanted. We knew it was going to be a challenge, but Kip and I were very clear with each other. When we had learned what we faced, we were smart enough to know what choices we had, and we weighed the outcomes of those choices. Above all, neither she nor I felt we were being forced to choose this particular path. We both believed in each other and we wanted to do this.

My parents were not so sure, but they at least went with us to meet Kip's parents.

The reception there was a bit different.

"Christ! Janette Ann Hurley, I am ashamed of you. If you were going to get yourself pregnant, you could have chosen a **Man** to do it with, and not this **Boy**." Her mom emphasized the words "Man" and "Boy" as she scowled at me to make her point. Then she turned to my parents.

"Well, thank you, Mr. and Mrs. Hendrickson. We can take it from here. She will have an abortion and that will be that. Good day."

"NO!"

Kip and I pleaded, promised, argued, and begged, but it was to no avail. When I realized that we were making no progress, I made an announcement.

"Well, we don't really need any of your help or support anyway! We do not want an abortion! So, although we know it will be hard to do this alone, that is what we will do. So there! Right, Kip?"

"That's right! It's my body, I love this man, and no matter what you or dad think, we are going to get married and have a wonderful family!"

We were at an impasse, but time was not really a problem. We had some weeks before we really needed to do anything drastic. I allowed myself to be dragged home by my parents and I called Kip to see how she was holding up.

Her mother answered the phone.

"Kip is not here. She told me she does not want to see you. Good Lord, child. If she wanted to see anyone it would be a real man, not you!"

Then she hung up.

I had taken the fast lane straight to Hell. Calling, going to her house, sending letters, pounding on her door, or yelling at the sky only confirmed that she was not there. There was no way to talk with her – cell phones would not be invented for another 35 years. Kip did finally call me 10 days later to break up with me. She said she did not love me, and quickly hung up.

I never saw Kip again. She went somewhere else to attend high school. I never had a chance to speak to her or learn where she had gone. I found out later that she had the abortion four days after our last meeting. Her mother sent my parents the medical bill (even though the procedure was illegal at the time). I heard that she married a doctor a few years later. And I went to work at the Goodyear store to earn the money to pay for the abortion I never wanted in the first place.

I do not know if it was to be a boy or a girl. I had a vasectomy when I turned 20. I told the doctors it was because my brother had a terrible congenital disease, and I did not wish to face my child having it. I do not know, even now, if that was the truth, but the excuse served its purpose. I never made another child. That was the only one. I will never know about the life that might have been.

This is the emptiness of a parent who has lost a child. Sometimes this may happen before they are born, as in this case, and sometimes after it happens after the child has lived and died too young. It is a pain I cannot share with others because at the word "abortion," they assume that I am the monster. I just don't go there.

I still love them both, Kip and my unborn child, but it is a story with a definite end, after all.

I found Kip again in 2009. She was living in Texas and still playing her guitar and singing along with some other, big-name musicians who would be familiar to anyone in the Austin Music Scene. We talked on the telephone twice. The second time we spoke, I learned that her cancer had returned, and she didn't have long to live. We never spoke again.

Kip died in 2010 from cancer while living in Austin, Texas. She was survived by her significant other, Arlo, and one child, a girl. Kip's daughter was born in 1972, three years after we split. She was the doctor's child, not mine.

4

LUNACY

Earthrise

By William Anders, Apollo 8 Astronaut. December 1968

After Kip, I spent the next couple of years in an alcohol- and drug-induced haze while going to Spring Branch High School in Houston. I do not know if this was my reaction to the whole situation with Kip, my general rebellion as a teenager, or my exploration of my own boundaries (how much could I get away with and still be okay?). My junior and senior years at Spring Branch were strange, even by my standards. I do remember having relationships with many girls, but I barely remember any details. I drank during school hours when I wasn't tripping on some other highly illegal or dangerous substance. There is nothing positive to say about that part of my life, except to say that I survived it. Somehow.

I do not glorify these times because I am not proud of the person I was and because, occasionally, I got my fingers burned. One day, I overdosed on pain pills in drafting class, and I was carried down to the nurse's office. The school administrators called the police, and the nurse called my dad. I only remember waking up and seeing my father and a police officer in a heated discussion about who would take me out of there.

My dad won the argument. Later that same day I was at the hospital, beside my brother's bed holding a catch basin. I had chosen to overdose myself on pain pills on a day when my brother was scheduled to have an eye operation. The outcome of that episode could have gone either way. My story might have ended right there if I had been sent to jail. I know of others who were not as lucky as me. For some reason, I seemed to be lucky when I needed it. At other times, I was just careful enough.

My luck held, and in May of 1971, I graduated in the top 25% of my high-school class. Because of my class standing and a blisteringly high score on my SAT, I was offered a slot in the Honors Program as the University of Houston. I started classes in the fall of 1971 with a major in general studies.

Both students and faculty in the University of Houston Honors Program were genuinely impressive. The students were smart, of course, but they were also free-spirited, self-confident, and sexually active. For the first time in my life, I felt like I belonged somewhere. I spent three years in the breakroom of the Science Building being challenged by my fellow students and professors as never before. One day it might be a new sorting routine for the computer science department. The next day it was a complicated math problem or a test of the para-psychic talents of flatworms. Then, when all the day's challenges were placed aside, we would pile into our cars (I still had the 1962 Volkswagen) and head over to someone's house for chili and long necks. Later in the evening, there might be chemistry explosions in the garage, kite flying in a Houston thunderstorm, or picking your partner and disappearing. This was 1972, and the sex was easy and pretty much harmless compared to what dating life would soon become. AIDS and other truly vicious STDs were not prevalent yet.

There was one thing that soon became clear to me about the Honors Program. I felt like I belonged with these kinds of people. I had never met anyone, much less a room full of people, who could challenge me academically and ask me questions that I could not answer. I was in "Bob Heaven."

Yes, I was having a great time, but it was still not enough. I continued to be dogged by the feeling that I had this great "talent," and since it was an accident of birth that it had come to me, I felt that I must owe it to someone to use it "appropriately." This feeling of unworthiness was a heavy burden as I approached my 21st birthday with no idea at all what I would do with this "enormous potential." As a result, I was doing poorly at the university – my grades were nowhere near where they should have been. I had huge dreams and a core belief that I needed to do something with my life, but absolutely no idea what that might be. In later years, I would learn from my aviation contacts that this was called "all airspeed and no heading."

Here I am, at age 19, still trying to "find myself."

One particularly lovely spring day in 1974, I was lying on the lawn at school, contemplating my future. Money had never been a motivator for me, but the chronic lack of it was wearing thin. It was difficult earning enough money to go to college and to be a full-time student at the same time. I was carrying 19 hours in the Honors Program and working 66+ hours a week at my pool hall. I was tired. As I lay there contemplating these facts, I could see where my life choices were leading me, and I didn't like it at all. I did not wish to work like this all my life.

Springtime was always a difficult time for me, and it still is. Perhaps I feel down because it only comes after what seems like the endless darkness and killing cold of the long winter. Still, spring also brings rebirth and that gives me hope I can just start everything over. I feel I can begin anew and all that is past is only a prelude to what lies ahead of me. Spring is the season when anything is possible, and it beckons me. Maybe it's just the warm sun after the cold of winter. I have always responded to that. Spring always seems to be the time that I drag my life out, inspect it (with all its warts and imperfections), and decide if it is still serviceable, or if I need to change it. I always seem to make my changes in the spring. Most of my relationships end or begin in the spring.

For a twenty-year-old college student with no debt, starting over was easy. Just drop out. In the Honors Program, there were psychology majors who might call it "impulsivity." If I called it anything, I just called it "wanderlust." Whatever. Dropping out seemed like a good thing to do, and I was just irresponsible enough that it took no more thought than that. I sold all my worldly possessions for $84.50 and set out on my Honda 350 motorcycle, headed west on Interstate 10.

A little to the west of San Antonio in Texas's hill country is a small ranching town named Uvalde. Driving north from there, about 30 minutes on U.S. Route 83, there's a little gem named Garner State Park. Garner is one of the best-kept secrets in Texas. It is situated on the beautiful Frio River in the Texas Hill Country. Lucky visitors there can swim in the river's crystal waters, enjoy some of the best barbeque to be found anywhere, or just take one of the many hiking trails up Mt. Baldy to see the great view.

I cannot now remember which of the high points behind Mt. Baldy I picked, but I hiked up there with a sleeping bag, a small tent, and some extremely forgettable food. I pitched my tent far from the other park-goers and sat down on a convenient rock. The view was lovely, and springtime in that part of Texas was cool and fair. I could see for miles from my vantage point, and I had absolutely nothing to do but think. It was just what I needed, and I sat there alone, taking in that view for three days.

It was in this place that I discovered the misplaced comma in my life's computer code – the reason my life was stuck. I discovered the reason I was running in an endless circle and stuck in the mire of poor decisions.

As I sat there, I wondered why it was that I had had all those jobs and yet was never fired or asked to leave any of them. Not once! For a wide variety of reasons, I had always chosen to move on to something new and different. I was only 20, yet I had never failed at any of the many jobs I had held.

Why had I left them? I wondered.

I was not challenged intellectually. I needed to be around people who were more like me. I mostly did every one of those jobs in my sleep.

Among the jobs that I had done, what was I incapable of?

Well, nothing! Had I ever come across a job that I could not do? The answer was no.

However, I realized that everything positive in my life had been possible ONLY IF I had been willing to pay the price to have it. I had to decide WHAT I wanted to do, make a plan on how I could get it, and do it!

So, first, I asked myself, *"Why **not** do something?"*

Well, because everything comes with a price and a payback.

So, what was the price?

Sometimes the price was low pay. Sometimes the price was danger. Sometimes the price was something else entirely and, frankly, sometimes the price was too high, but I could do it if I were willing to pay that too-high price. Whether or not some job made the cut came down to a formula:

Payback – Price = Quality of Job (for me)

Maximize the quality of the job, and I will find what I seek.

So, first, if I am willing to pay the price, I really can do anything. Right? Well, yes.

Great! So I can do almost anything if the payback is high enough to make the effort worthwhile. Let's try that as a test and see how it works …

How about a Doctor? No. Price too high.

Lawyer? Same thing. It would cost my integrity.

Politician? Ditto

Scientist? What subject? Besides, the cost is years of study and no excitement.

Logger? 6 feet tall and 135 pounds, I am not big enough.

Hippie? Been there.

General Dropout? Done that.

Pusher? Got the T-shirt.

Crap! I must have run the circle of these questions and answers a million times, and the price I computed was always higher than the potential payoff. I wanted something exciting, with enough pay to live on, that could make a difference in the world, and, and, and … what? Time passed. I was starting to get hungry. Days passed, and I was no closer to an answer. I needed inspiration! But I wasn't ready yet. There was something else I had to figure out first. What?

Then, slowly, it began to dawn on me that I was asking the wrong question.

If I can indeed do anything, then the right thing to ask myself would be this:

"Assume that I could do anything at all. <u>What would make me happiest</u>?"

How about a grand adventure that paid well? Hmmm! Tell me more ....

I was close. I knew it. It felt as if my inspiration were about to arrive. The anticipation was making me dizzy. And as I sat there in the gathering gloom, contemplating the valley below and watching how the deepening shadows slid across the valley floor in front of me, there, beyond the Frio River, above the dusty, scrubby hills, and all of the cactus in West Texas, the Moon began to rise over the ridge.

The Moon!

I was thunderstruck. It was as if I could see my entire life in that instant, and suddenly I knew with absolute clarity what I needed to do. I would walk on the Moon. Of course, I was much too late to be the first. But that's okay. NASA was going to need people like me. I did not want to do it for fame nor for accolades. No! In the best tradition of Sir Edmund Hillary, I was going to the Moon simply because it was there!

I knew the price would be high. As high as I could imagine, but the payoff would be the greatest adventure I could envision! Walking on the Moon and using my damned gift for the good of everyone was a goal that was worthy of the price I had to pay to achieve it!

This was the first time in my life that I had committed myself to anything so large, so audacious, and so bold. I knew it would take all of me and more, but now I had something to sink my teeth into that I would be proud to accomplish ... if I could.

As I rode my motorcycle back to Houston, I mapped out my plan for becoming a Moon-walking astronaut. Working backward, I knew that NASA loved test pilots. So, I would be a test pilot. I knew I would face stiff competition along the way, so I had to modify that goal just a bit. I had to be *the best* test pilot. Well, that meant that I would first need to be an outstanding military pilot! Top of my class and all that. But even before that, I needed a college degree to become an officer. My 53 academic hours completed with a 2.8 GPA was not a good start along those lines. Also, I knew I was sick to my teeth of being poor. I needed another way.

I thought of my friend, Bobby Sowders. He had enlisted in the Air Force, and on one of his early leaves from training, he had been back home. He told me of a scholarship called the Airman Education and Commissioning Program (AECP). The selectee is sent to the university of his or her choice and paid as an E-4 while attending the Air Force Reserve Officer Training Corps (AFROTC) commissioning program. While in school, the student is still on active duty and accrues pay and privileges along the way.

At the completion of their degrees, newly commissioned officers could compete for a pilot slot, if there were any. That was perfect! I knew there were only a couple of hundred scholarships for the whole Air Force, and there were no guarantees for any of this. *No problem!* I thought. I could roll the dice with anyone!

I even knew right away what I wanted as a major. I would choose computer sciences because, clearly, the computer would be how the new generation of spaceships would be operated. Having the right technical degree would make the difference for me in the selection processes that came later.

So, my path was clear, if somewhat barren of details. I would return to Houston, clean up my act, enlist in the Air Force, get one of those scholarships, become a pilot, get selected for Test Pilot School, become the best test pilot in the test pilot place (wherever that was), and get chosen to be an astronaut because I was so good. Then because I was the best astronaut, I would get selected to go to the Moon. Simple. If John Glenn could do it, I could do it. Right?

My 20-year-old ego swallowed that without even a second thought. Man, for such a smarty pants, I still had a lot to learn!

5

LEARNING THE BASICS

Flight 112 Squad leaders in front of our Barracks

I am second from the left.

W hen I returned to Houston, I was a man with a plan. I went by the recruiter's office to speak with him about enlisting with the intention of claiming one of the AECP scholarships so that I might become a pilot. He must have thought I was crazy, but he scheduled me for the aptitude tests for entry into the Air Force.

The enlisted aptitude tests in 1974 consisted of four sections with the highest possible score of 95 on each section. When my scores came back from the testing agency, my recruiter showed up at my front door with an amazed look on his face. I had scored 95-95-95-95.

For me, scores like that were what I expected. That was my great ego, and it was also my great flaw that I expected those kinds of results as if they were a given.

When I had returned to Houston, days before, I moved back in with a girl I had been living above in the house we shared with two other students. Her name was Joni Marlene Rice.

Joni and I were sleeping together when the mood struck us. After all, she lived just below me in the room downstairs. At other times I went my way, and she went hers. Under the strange rules of 1974, we had a bit of a relationship. She asked me why I was enlisting. I was straight and honest and told her that this was my plan for going to the moon. She listened and did not say much.

In the meantime, I started running and working out because I had a general idea that this was what would be required of me when my time came up to go to basic training.

When my date to go came up, I said good-bye to everyone, and went to Lackland Air Force Base (AFB) in San Antonio, Texas for USAF Basic Training.

As soon as our bus arrived on Lackland, our world changed immediately.

A very imposing Tech Sergeant stepped onto the bus and bellowed, "Welcome to Lackland! Get off the bus and drop all of your baggage in that pile over there! Keep any medications and leave the rest! Then enter the building labeled Welcome Center and proceed to the auditorium! You have five minutes! Go!"

We did our best to do as we were told, but there are always a few ....

"What are you LAZY people doing sitting down? You haven't earned the right to sit down! Get up! Get back on the bus and we will try it all again! You have two minutes!"

We ran back to the bus and got into our seats as quickly as we could, but again, there are always a few ....

Bam! The bus door slammed shut.

"What are you fat little boys doing hanging around outside my wonderful, beautiful, Air Force Blue bus? Everybody out! Get in the auditorium! You have one minute! Go!"

It took us over an hour just to enter the auditorium and sit down. It took another couple of hours for us, as individuals, to respond to our name, stand, read our last name, first name, middle initial, Social Security number, and hometown (from a card they had given us), and sit down.

We, as new recruits, did not understand why we were run through this hell. We only felt a sense of Us-vs-Them, and soon we were beginning to band together to help each other get through. This is exactly what the instructors wanted.

The instructors didn't do this because they enjoyed belittling recruits. They had very specific reasons for what they did, and it was their duty to transform us from undisciplined civilians into high-performing, well-trained airmen. They did it well. For instance, it is a basic principle of psychology that people will value something more highly if they are required to sacrifice more to get it. This is so basic that a rigorous initiation process is an important ritual for acceptance into college fraternities, sororities, and military basic training, just to name a few.

The recruit is learning every minute in basic training. Among the skills we internalized and lessons we learned were:

1. Listen to orders carefully and with absolute discrimination. If your commander says enter the room, but does not say to sit down, you may assume there

is a reason. Do what you are told. Don't improvise, unless specifically given permission to do so; and . . .

2. You cannot help but come to know your fellow recruits in this process. Who are the weak ones? Who are the aces? Which ones are good in military knowledge? Who are your brainiacs? These are your buddies for the next six weeks. It pays huge dividends to know who they are; and . . .

3. There are a million tricks to being a good soldier, like how to spit-shine a boot, or make a bed properly. Learn those where you can and when you can; but most of all . . .

4. Nobody gets through Basic Training or anything else of significance alone! A decent instructor will hold a recruit back for more training and might even remove him (or her) from specific job fields if they do not internalize this message. It is, by far, the most important thing that the recruit learns in basic training. Nothing in life and nothing in the military is done solo. You must rely on others to achieve anything significant.

After the hours-long "welcoming," we were all happy to be marching (well, walking close together, more or less in step) to the chow hall and then our barracks for a good night's sleep. We represented people from every corner of the country. We were city kids, country kids, curly headed or straight haired, all different colors of skin, and all different religions. We were all given the same goal and the same message on how to achieve that goal: Cooperate and Graduate.

We walked in step to the chow hall only to learn that the chow hall was closed! We had wasted too much time in the welcoming process. So, we walked in step, again, to our barracks. We learned later that NOBODY gets chow on their first night at Lackland.

It took us a number of tries to enter the barracks properly and get by the dorm guard. Much like the Welcome Center, we were required to recite a very specific litany which included our name and the last four digits of our Social Security number. If we messed it up, we went to the back of the line and tried again. The dorm guard was a recent graduate of the same Basic Training we were just starting. He assisted the instructors and did just what his job title said. He guarded our barracks.

We also met our Training Instructor (TI) – the man who would be in charge of us throughout our training. Once we were able to enter our barracks, the TI directed us to sit down in a circle. Then he spoke loudly and clearly:

"Welcome to MY United States Air Force. For the next six weeks, you and I are going to play a game. You see, as an enlisted man myself, I would not want you to call me Sir. I work for a living! However, you are going to need to practice this skill so you can clean up you dirty mouths. From now until your graduation, my first name will be Sir and your first name will be Airman."

I can remember even now, 40 years later, how odd the word sounded to me. Airman? I rolled it around on my tongue. Air Man. Aer Mann. Aor Monn. Air Mein. Airman.

Imagine. Here I was, day-one in USAF Basic Training, and I had never heard the term "Airman" before. When, about an hour later, he named me as one of the four squad leader positions in the 48-man flight, I could hardly act surprised. It was those damned test scores.

Of course, we did not eat or sleep that first night at all. When the bed-drills were not so bad as to embarrass the TI, we were allowed to sleep for about 10 minutes. And then, it was the start of day two.

Day two was very significant. It was the day we stopped being Rainbows and became Pickles. Rainbows were the multicolored mishmash of humanity that stepped off the bus on day one. Their hair was all different lengths, they were dressed in whatever they were wearing when they arrived, they were absolutely helpless, and they needed other airmen to guard their dorm for them. Rainbows cannot march and they all act like individuals. A Pickle is a Rainbow who has started their transformation. Pickles all look alike. Pickles have no name or rank. Pickles are wonderfully uniform in their green fatigues and buzzed haircuts. The whole idea is to strip the recruit of their old identity and build a new one.

We started our second day by marching (as best we could) to the Big Green Machine. This was a massive building at Lackland – it just happened to be painted green. This was the facility where young men were first given their buzz haircut and were issued all of their uniform items, like fatigues, boots, black socks, low quarter shoes, and powder blue uniforms. They also receive wash cloths, toiletries, and so on. Women also go through the same Big Green Machine process, but their training is conducted separately from the men.

Then when new airmen emerge from the other end of the Big Green Machine, they all look in the crowd of strangers for a familiar face, not fully realizing this *is* their flight. Nobody looks familiar because the transformation from Rainbow to Pickle is so dramatic and complete that it is not until they begin to speak that regional accents and vocal patterns start to come through and they re-learn who these people are.

It is only at this point, on day two, that the recruit begins to realize this life is very different from what it was in the outside world. Race means nothing anymore. Likewise, religion, your family's national origin, ethnicity, political affiliation, economic status, or birth order aren't important in this environment. They all mean nothing here. Here, the new airmen will be judged by their work ethic and the content of their character and nothing else. The recruit may have come in search of a new beginning, but what they receive is even more: a new chance to start fresh. For me, this was the first time in my life I felt that I had found a family. I would be starting fresh with no prior history, and that suited me just fine.

As I marched back to the barracks and I watched an autumn rain shower splash and splash on the seemingly bald head in front of me, I was happy.

6

A GOOD THING TO DO ON A THURSDAY

Joni Marlene

About half-way through Basic Training, at the end of week three, we got our first break. I went to the bowling alley and phoned my friend Bobby Sowders to tell him I had been smiled upon by my TI and that he, Bobby, could come on down to the bowling alley now to visit. We had arranged the visit one week before and I was looking forward to seeing him. When he arrived, two people got out of his car. Joni had driven up from Houston with him to see me.

The three of us bowled a few frames and talked about this and that. Then Joni broke her news to me. After talking about the opportunities in the Air Force, she had decided to enlist, too!

"Why did you do that?" I asked her, not sure if she was serious or not.

"Seemed like a good thing to do on a Thursday," she joked.

I just stared at her in disbelief.

"Besides, that opens some possibilities for us."

"What do you mean?" I asked.

"Well, I know that you hate being poor and I also know that you don't really like to live in the dorms," she explained. "There's a program my recruiter told me about that will take care of both of those things if we work together."

"Go on." I was skeptical.

"We could get the Air Force to pay us a lot more money and we would get to choose our jobs and where we want to go for our assignments," she continued.

"What are you talking about? I don't understand." I was still not sure what she was getting at.

"It's a program called Join Spouse. If you get into the program, you don't have to live in the dorms. You both draw separate rations and separate housing, so you make out. I don't want to live in the dorms, do you?"

"No, I really don't." It was true. I didn't want to live in the dorms. No one really does.

"And having first pick at your assignment doesn't suck, either!" She had completed her argument.

"So, what does your recruiter say?"

"I don't know," she answered. "You want me to ask?"

"Sure," I replied. "But, just to be clear, we need to get married for all of this to work? Right?"

"Yes."

"Well, let me know what the recruiter says."

And I stepped to the line and rolled a gutter ball.

Looking back, I should have taken that as an omen ....

I was a little weirded-out by the whole thing.

"I think I just proposed to Joni. That was strange."

CROSSING

As I walked back to my barracks, I put all thoughts of what just happened at the Lackland Bowling Alley out of my mind. I had work to do.

Joni and I were married almost a year later, in December of 1974. I was home on leave, and this was the opportune time as I had just finished an eight-month technical training school at Lowry AFB in Denver, Colorado and she was just getting ready for basic training at Lackland. After the wedding, we drove to Luke AFB just west of Phoenix, Arizona. We moved into a two-bedroom apartment near the base, and we had plenty of money left over because we were authorized "Married Drawing Separate Rations" and "Separate Housing" allowances. The money was good, the job was great, and I should have been happy. The only fly in the ointment was Joni.

When she got her first opportunity to use the telephone from Lackland, she called me on the phone.

"Hello, Bob?"

"Oh, hi Joni! Good to hear from you. How is everything going?"

"I hate his place." She was angry. "I hate the Air Force. And I hate you for talking me into this. I am going to make you pay for this."

She was good to her word – she completed her Air Force commitment – which kept us together because of the Join Spouse Program. We had more money than our enlisted friends, and yet, I was focused on other things.

Wedding photo of Joni and Me
The dress is the same dress my mother wore at her wedding.

My job in the Air Force was to be a Weapons Control System (WCS) mechanic at Luke AFB. That was a lot better than it sounded like. I was not a mechanic, at all. Being a WCS mechanic actually meant I was responsible for all of the weapons systems on the McDonnell Douglas F-4C/D Phantom II. This was a dream job for me. It combined working on radar and computers on a front-line Mach 2 Jet Fighter.

The training at Lowry gave me an unexpected leg up on understanding computers and the amazing people who built them. Once again, I was discovering that the people who had invented the early computers were very clever, and I greatly appreciated that. Early computers were astronomically expensive, were slow and had limited memory. How problems were solved by a machine depended very heavily on understanding the capabilities and the limitations of that machine. The techniques I learned in this job, which were ten years old already, would illuminate my understanding of how these things worked and make my path through college that much easier.

Once at Luke, I worked through the advanced sections of my training and finally achieved the level of proficiency to work by myself on the flight line. It was now time for me to initiate the next step of my plan to walk on the Moon. I had to seek permission to take the Air Force Officer Qualifying Test (AFOQT).

In the Summer of 1976, I was given the go-ahead to take the test. Compared to the test for becoming an enlisted airman where I had done so well, this test was more difficult; it also came in five parts. Once again, the highest score possible on each section was 95.

I was at work on the flight-line when I heard from the Consolidated Base Personnel Office (CBPO) that my scores were back. I got on my Honda 550 motorcycle and went right over to see if I was competitive. I walked through the main door and approached an airman at the duty desk.

"Hello. My name is Bob Hendrickson. I understand that my AFOQT scores are back."

"Oh yeah. Just a minute."

I heard him walk to the back and whisper to one of his colleagues behind a partition.

"He's here. That guy I was telling you about."

"Who? The General?" came the female reply.

"Yeah," he said.

The young airman came around the side of the partition. She had a piece of paper in her hand.

"You're Sergeant Hendrix?" She asked.

My heart skipped a beat, wondering if there even was a Sergeant Hendrix on Luke AFB.

"Hendrickson?" I prompted her.

She looked at the paper in her hand. "Oh, yeah. Hendrickson." She handed me the paper.

43

"Damnedest thing I ever have seen. You're gonna be a General someday!" she exclaimed.

I thanked her and I took the paper. 95-95-90-95-95. *Damn,* I thought. *I wonder what I missed?*

Then I walked out to the parking lot, got on my motorcycle, and did wheelies right out of the parking lot.

The next day, I returned to my commander's office and requested permission to meet the board of officers that would make the final officer training selections. The selection board would be looking at me, not my scores. The test scores did not hurt, but they did not close the deal at all. If the selection board of five officers did not think I had the leadership potential or the maturity to be an officer, the test scores would not mean a thing. In short, I had to put on a good show.

Once again, my gift for selling myself to a board of officers came through for me and I as one of 65 selectees Air Force-wide for the Fall 1976 AECP (The fully- paid-for commissioning Program.). I was going to be an officer.

Months later, I was all set. My bags were packed, and I was ready to travel to the University of Texas at Austin (UT) to finish a degree in Computer Sciences, beginning that fall. All I needed was a set of orders. When the congressional budget for 1976 came out, I and 64 other enlisted people were dismayed. Because of post-Vietnam budget cuts, Congress had eliminated funding for all the AECP commissioning slots!

Just like a bowling pin, I had been set up only to be knocked down again. But, as before, I figured there was one more way to skin that cat. I had never heard of it, and I do not know if it was ever offered before or since 1976, but I learned about the Air Force Scholarship and Commissioning Program (ASCP). In this program, the participant was discharged from the Air Force and had to pay his or her own way back to school. The program provided $100 per month and books for the scholar. However, if the recipient had eligibility for the GI Bill, which I did by this time, they could use the proceeds from that to make tuition and living expenses more palatable.

The Air Force guaranteed me five semesters at The University of Texas at Austin (UT) to complete a degree program and graduate. That sounded considerably worse than the sweet deal provided for the other program which paid me. It was not great, but I had the choice to take this opportunity or wait until next year and see if things changed.

Qualifying for the paid commissioning program automatically qualified me for the ROTC based program, so all I had to do was allow the Air Force to discharge me early, sign a contract that stated I would return in five semesters (if the Air Force even needed me at that time), and there was no guarantee I would have a pilot slot on my return.

It was a huge gamble. There were so many things that could go wrong. By this time in my life, I was used to taking my chances.

I rolled the dice.

This time, It came up a winner!

I graduated from The University of Texas at Austin in December 1978 with a bachelor's degree in Computer Sciences (With Honors) and that all-important slot to Air Force Pilot Training. Along the way, I carried a 4.0 GPA in Computer Sciences and 3.6 GPA overall. I was selected the AFROTC Cadet of the Year for the State of Texas, chosen as Corps Commander of the Air Force ROTC detachment at UT, designated commander of the Air Force, Navy, and Army detachments for the Presidential Review, and performed so well I earned Distinguished Graduate honors. Soon, I was back on active duty and off to Undergraduate Pilot Training (UPT) in the class slated to graduate as the 7th class in 1980, 80-07.

During the years I was at the University of Texas at Austin, most of the pilot candidates in ROTC across the nation were, at one time or another, faced with a stark choice because of an Air Force-wide reduction in force . This meant that unless they were one of the top performers nationwide, they lost their pilot training slot. Each Cadet who was affected by this had to decide whether to continue with their Air Force scholarships knowing they would not become a pilot upon graduation, but rather be assigned as a ground support officer of some kind because of the overage of pilots currently serving in the Air Force. There had to be a reduction of pilot candidates in the pipeline. That flexibility in the pipeline was provided by the cadets in ROTC..

I was lucky. I was already "prior enlisted" because of my two years spent at Luke and I was older, too, so it was a bit easier for me to hold on to some of the top positions in the Corps. As long as I kept my grades up, I was able to hold on to my pilot slot by the skin of my teeth.

Meanwhile, throughout my Air Force career, Joni was proud to tell her friends that she had never once saluted her officer husband. She thought it was beneath her to do so. She disrespected me and all of my colleagues along the way, even knowing that in the 1970's and 1980's an officer's social life was critical to his career success. I only got a pass on her behavior because she made no secret to any of my commanders that she did these things specifically to torpedo my career. As a result, I was treated somewhat like a single officer and I was allowed to excuse my wife from participating in the otherwise required social functions.

7

UPT

Here I am returning from one of the required solo flights in the Cessna T-37B "Tweet" – USAF Primary Jet Trainer in 1980.

UPT was an exercise in taking a drink from a fire-hose. When students were flying equipment that costs so much to operate, Air Force instructors simply could not waste a lot of time trying to remediate student weaknesses. If a student pilot (stud) got airsick, they might be given two or three rides to get that under control – if they could not, they would be kicked out of the program. If a stud failed a check ride at the end of a section of training (there were six sections), they would be given a re-test. If they failed that, they would be kicked out for cause. Some studs got into the cockpit and realized that it is far different from what they had expected, and they quit, or "SIE" (Self-Initiated Elimination). When I was in UPT from 1979-80, the overall pass rate was only about 66%. On the first day of training, when the studs showed up to the classroom, an instructor stood up in the front of the class and said, "Congratulations. Welcome to class 80-07, United States Air Force Undergraduate Pilot Training. You are now among the most elite groups of people anywhere in the world. You have passed so many hurdles to get here at all, you should be proud. However, the fun is just beginning. If you will, look to your left. Now look to your right. In one year, two of you will graduate, and the other will not. Which are you?" The pressure was on.

It's one of the primary functions of military pilot training to apply stress to the student to see if they can perform under pressure. The instructor pilots (IPs) in my class would yell at the stud if they made the smallest mistake and would demand better when the stud finally performed the maneuver satisfactorily. I actually had one IP, a no-nonsense captain who had flown fighters in Vietnam, grab my oxygen hose and yank my head to make sure I was looking at what he wanted me to see!

As the stud got deeper into the program, the IP might lighten up a bit, but not much. This pressure-filled approach is important for a military pilot who will fight and live or die from his airplane. The student must demonstrate calm, measured responses to stressful situations every day to pass this test. The best pilots in the world would be useless if they fell apart in a crisis.

Every morning in the T-37 and T-38 flight phases of UPT (as opposed to the initial academic phases), an IP from the Flight Safety Office would come into the class ready room and begin with the morning briefing, touching on some topic of interest like fuel management or something. No jeopardy there.

But then it would begin ....

"Okay. For today's scenario, you are flying your T-37, solo, out in the practice area. You are just pulling through the top of a loop when you hear a loud bang. What do you do ... Lieutenant Hendrickson?"

I would be required to stand up from my chair, at full attention, and respond to the scenario.

"Sir, I would maintain aircraft control and investigate by first scanning my flight instruments and then my engine instruments. What do I see?"

"Okay, your flight instruments indicate that you are wings level, inverted, with an airspeed of 100 knots. Engine instruments indicate normal for your right engine, but your left engine indicates a fire and zero rpm."

"Sir, I would continue to exercise aircraft control by applying a bit of right rudder to keep the nose pointed straight so that I can avoid inducing any yaw. This will ensure that I do not develop the pre-requisite for a spin. I would monitor my airspeed. When I see at least 150 knots on the downhill side, I would roll right side up and trim the airplane, (trimming the airplane makes it easier to fly.). Then I would perform the boldface items for engine fire which are: **THROTTLE – IDLE, FUEL LEVER – CUTOFF, FIRE HANDLE, -PULL.**"

"Okay, Lieutenant Hendrickson, Sit down."

His eyes went around the room, finally stopping on his next target.

"Lieutenant Jones."

"Yes, sir!"

"Unfortunately, your T-37 begins to spin. What do you do?"

And it continued from there ....

The stud had to remain at attention, use all the customs and courtesies required when speaking to a superior officer. The stud had to be right, and when the time came to quote from the Emergency Procedures, they had to be letter-perfect.

All of this was done in front of everybody in my class and all our instructors. The reward for successfully running through a five-minute ordeal like this was that the stud was allowed to fly on that day. If they got anything wrong, like saying "Fuel Switch" instead of "Fuel Lever," or failing to select the correct maneuver, the student would spend an entire day, humiliated, sitting at his desk studying the Flight Handbook instead of flying. It was the most stressful few minutes of every day, but young studs learned a lot about themselves and their limits from that.

U.S. Air Force Undergraduate Pilot Training, Assignments Night, Class 80-07, Williams AFB, AZ.

It was Assignments Night, and our class was just days from pinning on our new USAF pilot wings. This was huge – our follow-on flying assignment would determine the course of our Air Force career. Each one of us had a great deal, personally and professionally, riding on what happened.

The students from our sister class were on the stage at the Williams AFB Officer's Club east of Mesa, Arizona on this random Friday night near the end of our year long, UPT class. I was finishing fourth in my class of 56. Not the best, but certainly good enough to qualify for what I wanted.

The obligatory "I Love Me" picture where I am posed on the supersonic Northrop T-38A "Talon" USAF Advanced Jet Trainer

I had requested to fly the F-4 Phantom as my follow-on assignment from UPT. My old flame from my enlisted days was still a front-line, twin-engine, supersonic fighter jet that had a cool factor that was over-the-top! Every class prior to ours had received between 6 and 10 F-4s per class on their Assignments Night, so my plan was proceeding like clockwork. I felt I had not even gotten to the hard part yet.

The tradition at Williams AFB was that some of the students from our sister class would set up a table on the stage at the officers' club. With the assignment for each pilot written on a piece of paper and sealed in an envelope, the envelopes were stacked neatly on the table. The club was full of spouses, parents, and well-wishers, each of whom had an emotional interest in what was about to happen.

The IPs in charge of the ceremony would open one envelope, read the name aloud, and pour a shot of Kentucky Bourbon for each engine as the recipient would march to the stage. The recipient would down his required shot(s), receive his assignment, read it to the crowd and endure the typical military jibes, catcalls, and jeers (and cheers) of those assembled.

By this time, just days from the end of the class, most of the students knew each other very well, they knew each other's preferences, and there were very few surprises. So, it was a fun night, we all got drunk and celebrated each other's success at just graduating from a program that had a washout rate of nearly thirty percent.

When my name was read, the guys on stage poured my two shots and watched as I came forward. I went on stage, drank my two shots, held out my hand, and watched incredulously as they silently filled the two shot glasses again. I looked at their faces questioningly. One of them looked at me with a mixture of compassion and sadness and quietly said, "Drink 'em, Bob."

I turned and looked at my classmates in the audience and saw shock in their eyes, too. I realized that the entire club was silent, expectant, waiting. *Four engines????*

I turned back to the table and stared at the shots. I looked at the three people on stage with me for some clue that it was a bad joke.

"Needs of the Air Force," one of them said, repeating the old cliché.

I slowly drank the additional shots, and held out my hand, again. I took the envelope, opened it, turned and read to the others in attendance:

"KC-135 to Dyess."

And just like that, my dream ended. I didn't even look at the KC-135 as a real weapons system. It was just an old tanker. A weak, lame version of the Boeing 707.

This was a direct slap in my face. My dream of walking on Mare Tranquillitatis (The Sea of Tranquility) was over in a second.

I had lost the Moon.

8

WHITE ANVILS

The supersonic Northrop T-38A "Talon" – the
USAF Advanced Jet Trainer

The white, honeycombed aluminum, a piece of the former T-38 flight control, was hot but not because of any heat from the recent fire. I dropped it back onto the hot, Arizona sand to be with its neighbors. I rubbed the sting from my fingers for the millionth time that day and cursed at no one in particular,

"Ouch! Shit. I don't know who would think this was a good place to put a runway. Whoever was responsible should get to pat the rattlesnakes and scorpions out here a while."

My thoughts trailed off as I studied a small, white, mis-shapen little piece of something at my feet. What caught my eye was that it seemed out of place. I nudged it with the toe of my boot, testing its weight. It did not weigh a lot. I wondered what it could be as I looked to my left, my right, and up and down the irrigation canal, trying to understand what it was and how it got here. It looked for all the world like a tiny chicken bone, but it was fresh.

"Yeah, that is definitely a bone, but what kind is it?"

Well, they said to pick up everything. I put it in my bag and forgot about it.

I did not know until very much later in the investigation the story that the little piece of bone had to tell.

It was early August 1980, the Monday after graduation weekend from UPT. My class of 80-07 had been celebrating for those three days, but now it was time for all of us to sober up and get back to some kind of work. At the time, in 1980, the Air Force was turning out about 100 pilots a month who would be flowing into yet another training class in their new airplane, whatever that was to be for them. Since these newly minted pilots could not all go to their next classes at once, many, like me, needed something to do for our 6- to 8-week wait before training started.

I chose to work at the flying safety office. The pilots who worked there amazed me. They were esteemed by everyone, including and especially the other instructor pilots. They seemed to know so much about why and how airplanes crashed. They knew why it was that sometimes the airplanes failed, and sometimes the pilots failed and why sometimes it was both, or neither. I was in awe of these pilots, and I wanted to learn what they knew.

Monday morning at 8:30, I was in the Flight Safety Office. I was given the mundane task of filing various manila folders in a metal filing cabinet. It was my very first day, and I had been there for all of 10 minutes when the major in command of the office ran through, grabbed his hat, and turned to me.

"Come on, Bob we are going to the crash site!"

"HUH? What crash? When? Where?"

I ran along behind him wondering what this was going to be like. All I could do was to try and keep up. We piled into his brown, Air Force issue pickup truck with yellow lights on the top and the smell of very old French Fries inside and bounced across three runways and out the gate by the end of the runway.

Even this early in the morning, the sun was well up in the sky and the heat was making the short, brown corn in the field where the T-38 had crashed wilt even more. About fifty feet beyond the gate was a pillar of the blackest smoke I had ever seen in my life. It was so thick that it almost appeared to be a solid column. We had arrived at the moment two huge fire trucks began pumping water on the surprisingly small fire – it didn't take long to extinguish it.

As a brand-new second lieutenant pilot, I was not even close to being qualified to investigate the accident. I knew that, and I was not upset at all being an "extra" at this crash. What I did get to do, however, turned out to be a great opportunity for me to learn about the art of the investigation.

In the Air Force, anytime there is a crash involving a fatality or anything else considered significant, a mishap investigation board is formed to investigate the cause of the crash. This board will be made up of experts who are split into groups by specialty. For instance there might be an engine group, to see if there was any problem there. There also may be a flight controls group to look at aircraft flight controls. The structures group looks at pretty much everything mechanical on the aircraft. There is almost always a flight surgeon. Finally, there is always a Board President who oversees the investigation and leads all of the disparate specialists. Since I was not qualified to do any of those tasks, the board president designated me as the non-titled tag along who brought the donuts and coffee, and ran errands for the real investigators.

As the designated "Go-Fer" for the mishap investigation board, I was privileged to attend all the specialist portions of the investigation. For instance, I got to witness the flight control teardown where the experts took apart all the flight control actuators. (The control actuators are the devices that actually move the flight control surface. In the T-38 for example, they are all hydraulic.)

A flight control actuator on a T-38 can be thought of as a hollow pipe with a piston inside. When an aircraft crashes, the impact can cause the piston to leave a mark on the inside wall of the actuator. When it does, this is called a "Witness Mark." It tells the investigator precisely where the flight control was at impact. Good to know. Similarly, there may be witness marks on older style instruments where the needle might have slapped the case upon impact.

In this accident, these witness marks were exactly where they would be 0.5 seconds after being released from a cross-controlled stall.[1]

I also attended the engine teardowns with the engines group, which established that the throttle positions were fully forward, even though the engines themselves were just beginning to respond to the pilot's input and were barely producing above idle power. The expected engine thrust at this point in a properly flown final turn should have been around 75% power.

---

[1] When an airplane is in coordinated flight, meaning everything is pointed in the same direction, the flight controls agree with the direction of flight and are said to be coordinated. When the flight controls for some of the directions of flight are in disagreement, they are said to be uncoordinated, there is usually more drag on the airplane and it requires more power to remain aloft. For instance, in this case, it was found that this pilot was commanding the aircraft to turn right by the ailerons left down-right up, but at the same time needed some left rudder to keep the nose up. This is what is known as a cross-controlled stall. It is also the definition of a snap roll.

The tail of the T-38 involved in the accident[2]

I was allowed to accompany the investigators as they interviewed family members about the pilot's 72-hour history prior to the flight. I was permitted to observe the interviews and learn how to balance my emotions against the need for investigators to get the facts. Despite the raw emotional nature of some of the family members' interviews, we were able to establish that the young father piloting the plane that morning was exhausted after having stayed up through the previous night with a sick child.

I also attended the autopsy. Here I learned the story of the small bone I had found on the morning of the crash. Investigators identified this small piece of bone as

[2] This is a photo of the tail section which shows how the flight controls, particularly the rudder, tend to become trapped by the surrounding structure during the crash sequence, thus revealing a clue. It is the essence of the investigator's job to precisely know how important that clue might be, or was it a random event which means nothing?

a phalange, one of the finger's bones. From their years of experience, investigators specially trained in flight medicine (flight surgeons) knew something that I did not. The hands of a pilot who is still gripping the flight controls at impact are crushed by that impact. But this pilot's hands were not crushed. This pilot's fingers were all neatly sliced in half at the first phalanges bone of each finger! Why?

It took me several minutes to puzzle it out. The flight surgeon, having seen this before, waited while I thought about it. One more bit of information eventually gave me the final piece when the flight surgeon silently pushed the relevant page of the structures group across the table to me. It read "Witness marks and location of metal failures lead us to believe that the pilot's shoulder harnesses on his seat were not locked."

But I recalled the fact that his fingers weren't crushed. That indicated he was not flying the aircraft anymore. He was, in fact, attempting to eject from the plane. His hands were in the ejection handles on either side of his ejection seat and were neatly guillotined by the impact. The pilot had not had time to even raise the handles, which would have locked the shoulder harness. It was then that the full tragedy of this crash finally hit me, and I had to stop for a moment to get control of my own emotions.

"He had come so close!"

We had established why the airplane had crashed, how it had impacted, and how the force vectors had acted upon his body and told us more, and all of that was based on impersonal and dry science. But in order to fully understand the mishap, we had continued to dig and discovered his thought process down to the final instant, and how close he came to getting out.

Unfortunately, this pilot was doomed from the instant that the airspeed of his T-38 had decayed to the stall and he attempted to give it one more little tug to "get it around the corner," to line up his plane with the runway.

The final report blamed pilot fatigue as the primary reason for this crash, but now I knew so much more.

A very small crash site[3]

I was transformed by this experience. It is difficult to overstate how much it meant to me to see this tragedy laid out before me in all of its detail. My emotions were hurting. I needed to do something. I suddenly realized with absolute clarity what was important and what was not, for this person, in this place, at this time. I knew that with the benefit

---

[3]   The size of the crash site is usually a function of the forward speed of the airplane at the moment of impact. Small sites such as this one indicate a great energy component (because of the great fracturing of all of the airplane forward of the tail section) but a low forward speed.

of hindsight, I could identify those things that could have made a difference in his outcome and those that could not. There was very little room for opinion or human ego here.

Physics did not argue with this pilot.

Gravity did not take a holiday because he was a loving father.

Bernoulli's equations on lift were just as valid for him as for the terrible black birds that circled aimlessly over the crash site that day in August, 1980.

These were the cold, hard realities that I had to learn to live with, or they would kill me as certainly as they did this young man.

I also knew one more thing and it was, for me, the most important lesson of all. I knew I could make a difference with what I learned. I could not only keep myself a bit safer when I was piloting an airplane, but I could make flying, in general, safer by sharing my lessons with those in the aircraft industry who could make a difference. Baby steps, to be sure. But steps in the right direction, nonetheless. I had found the use for my great gift in a very unexpected place!

I was blind-sided, hooked by a calling that fell from the sky on that hot morning in Arizona. I might not become an astronaut, but I bet I can save a few lives here on earth, if I do it right!

When the investigation was over, the reports were printed and sent out, six weeks had passed, and it was time for me to go to Castle AFB to train in the KC-135. From that time forward, I knew that Aircraft Accident Investigation would play a role in my life.

I just did not know how or if I would ever be any good at it.

9

STEAM JETS

A Boeing KC-135A "Stratotanker"
Perfecting touch-and-go landings at Dyess AFB,
just outside of Abilene, Texas

I was still feeling pretty sorry for myself when I arrived at Castle AFB in Merced, California, in early 1981. Here at the base where all the crew training would take place for my new airplane, I was coming to grips with my life's new direction. My dreams of becoming an astronaut had been dashed with an assignment decision that banished me to tankers. It was a decision that I felt was cavalier and irresponsible. "Needs of the Air Force," indeed! I was heartsick at my loss, and for the first time in my life, I had encountered a thing so large that I could not move it by the force of my will.

I was only beginning to realize that I had to add one more thing to my "go for it!" life strategy. I was learning a harsh lesson about putting all my eggs in a single basket. I did not have a backup plan for when my primary plan blew away like dandelion thistles on the wind. I had no way of knowing at that point in my life that better days than I could imagine were still ahead of me. All I knew was that I hurt, and I mourned my loss. I wanted someone else to hurt as I did. I wanted to wallow in my pain and spread it around a bit. So, I started out by belittling the airplane itself.

To me, this old piece of junk was better off in the bone-yard. The KC-135 was a derivative of the first large jet aircraft from Boeing, the Dash 80. Its Dash 80 design was ground-breaking in 1953, but by 1981, it had been left behind long ago by faster, prettier, and sexier airplanes. The nascent fighter pilot inside me felt embarrassed to be seen in a four-engine gas tank, the likes of which my grandmother could fly. Besides, I had never heard of any pilot selected for Test Pilot School based on his record at flying a KC-135.

The KC-135 was officially called the Boeing "Stratotanker," but we all called her the "Steam Jet." We called her that, not only because of her age, but because of the way thrust was created by the engines. Engine technology in 1954 was stone knives and bearskins compared to today. The KC-135 "A"-model was equipped with four Pratt & Whitney J57 turbojet engines. Turbojet engines of the day were incredibly noisy, underpowered, and unreliable. Under normal circumstances, the J57 was only able to produce about 9,500 pounds of thrust at sea level, which was not enough thrust to make a heavyweight KC-135 take off from even the Strategic Air Command's huge 13,000-foot-long runways. Unfortunately, that was state-of-the-art in 1954. But Pratt &Whitney engineers had one more trick up their sleeve for the J57 engine.

Taking a page from Sir Isaac Newton, they applied his second law of motion (F = MxA, or Force equals Mass times Acceleration). In other words, if you want more thrust (Force), they needed to find a creative method to increase the mass of the air passing through the engine.

This solution was both brilliant and crazy. To put this crazy idea in action, the KC-135A was built with an extra tank right between the main landing gear wheels. This tank held 670 gallons of demineralized water. This water was sprayed or "injected" directly into the engine intake during the critical first two minutes of takeoff and climb. This air-water mix increased the mass of the air going through the engine and resulted in the engine being able to produce 11,500 pounds of thrust, which was just enough thrust to take off. Thus, the aircraft became affectionately known to everyone as the "Steam Jet."

Here I am preparing for takeoff in the right seat of a KC-135A Steam Jet

One of the most problematic byproducts of this water injection process was the extreme noise it created. The KC-135A was one of the noisiest airplanes in the world during a water-injected takeoff. The Pratt & Whitney J57 engines produced so much sonic vibration in their exhaust airflow that the tail sections of all KC-135A aircraft needed to be reinforced with metal bands around the tail structure. They looked like barrel hoops and they helped keep the planes from experiencing metal fatigue on the tail section of the airplane due to the extreme sonic vibrations.

Happily, even though I continued to feel bitter because of my bad luck at getting a tanker, I soon felt a grudging respect for this airplane and the individuals who flew and maintained her. She was a classic, after all. She did a magnificent job at what she was built for, and she was as honest as any machine built in 1955 ever was.

The Steam Jet's aircrews and maintainers were absolutely the most professional individuals I ever had the good fortune to work with in my life. As a group, they were among the most underappreciated airmen I have known in the Air Force. The public, our families, the Wing Staff, and just about anyone who did not understand the tankers' mission and how it was done, in all of its complexity, only knew what they saw. They saw an old, noisy, outdated, smoky, filling-station in the sky. They saw a plane they thought could barely get off the ground and never went into combat. They saw a support aircraft and saw what they thought were a number of guys on Easy Street loitering around her.

But, as a group, these "Tanker Toads" as we were called, operated their assigned airplane, sat their tours on Nuclear Alert (where they sat in the back of the briefing room, behind the bomber crews), and typically, received lower job-effectiveness ratings on their promotion rankings because they were considered support people. These men and women flew with precision and professionalism second to no airmen, anywhere. The KC-135A was an extremely demanding aircraft to fly and maintain, and it is a testament to these airmen that they made it look easy. It absolutely was not!

Today, the KC-135 has served the Air Force's air refueling needs for more than 60 years. It was the mainstay of all refueling needs for the Strategic Air Command's (SAC's) Nuclear Deterrent Force for decades and has been modified many times. All the old J-57 equipped aircraft have been re-engined with much more modern, powerful, and quiet engines such as the General Electric CFM56.

Eventually, I came to trust and even love flying the Steam Jet and working with the people who serve her. I still wear the badge of "Steam Jet Pilot" proudly.

After all, a Steam Jet saved my life one day in Austin, Texas.

10

SMOKE IN THE AIR

McDonnell Douglas RF-4C
Mach 2.5 Photo-Reconnaissance Aircraft

"Fire in Number 1."

Frank's voice in my headset was so calm that his message was lost to me for a moment. So calm, in fact, that I almost ignored him. What was that again?

"What?" I asked into my headset/microphone that was on a little boom near my lips. But, as I did so, I was also looking up at the overhead panel in the cockpit of my KC-135. It seemed like we were always losing generators during takeoff lately. Still, there was no indication that anything was amiss up there.

No, not a generator, I thought.

For just an instant, my eyes met those of Captain Richard (Rick) Packard, who was also checking the generator lights. Rick was the aircraft commander (AC), and I was the copilot (CP) for this outreach flight to Bergstrom AFB in Austin,

Texas. Our KC-135 unit at Dyess, the 917th Air Refueling Squadron (917 ARS), would occasionally send a tanker to other nearby units to familiarize them with our aircraft and procedures. This program was called "Business Effort" because many Air Force units in 1982 were trying to incorporate business models that talked about the necessity of supporting one's "customers." The RF-4Cs at Bergstrom were some of our customers, so there we were.

"We" were crew number S101. All Tanker crews within a squadron were numbered from 101, 102, 103, etc., and were given a letter denoting their status. For instance, an R crew was a "Regular" or "Mission Ready" crew. N was "non-qualified" (perhaps the Aircraft Commander needed a check ride). An E crew was an "Elite" crew – typically, it had an instructor assigned to the crew. But, among all of the crews, there were two S crews: S101 (the senior crew) and S102 (the junior crew). The S crews were the Select or Standards and Evaluation (Stan Eval) crews, meaning they were the crews who administered the check rides and academic testing to ensure all crews could perform the mission. As the co-pilot on S-101, I was the designated person to be a resident expert on and to teach aircraft performance to all assigned crews. I also administered check rides to Aircraft Commanders and COPILOTs in the simulator. So, as the S-101 Aircraft Commander, it's accurate to say that Rick Packard was the best pilot in the 917 ARS.

The date was August 6, 1982, and we were going home after we completed this last mission. After four days in Austin, this was to be our final flight out of Bergstrom. We were tasked to take off from Bergstrom and fly into their practice area, where we were to loiter and provide refueling for a number of RF-4C photo-reconnaissance jets for as long as we could. After we finished, we were to turn to make the short flight back to Dyess.

This mission profile matched mission profiles that tankers flew years later in support of wars like Operations Desert

Storm and Iraqi Freedom. In those conflicts, tankers in large numbers simply orbited outside the kill zones and refueled all allied airplanes sent to them by Airborne Warning and Control System (AWACS) aircraft – typically the Boeing E-3 "Sentry." So, we really did not know exactly how long our flight was to be. We were tasked to stay in the practice area until we ran out of fuel for receivers, or we ran out of receivers, whichever came first. The day before, during our mission planning for this flight, the commander of the host unit of RF-4C photo reconnaissance airplanes asked me how much fuel we could "bring to the party?"

"Well, sir," I replied, "your unit does not have any demineralized water, so this will be a dry takeoff; that is, no water injection will be available for us. That drops our takeoff weight by about 50 thousand pounds. With the weather expected and the calm wind affecting our maximum takeoff weight, and all of the other considerations, I think I can guarantee that we can arrive in the practice area with about eighty-thousand pounds of fuel available for your reconnaissance airplanes. Just remember, we also use the same fuel to keep our tanker aloft, so that eighty-thousand-pound capability we arrive with, decreases the longer we orbit in the area."

The fighter squadron commander was scribbling some notes as I was speaking. He stopped, momentarily. "So, for want of a little water, we lose 50 thousand pounds of fuel?"

"Well, yes," I said. "However, if we get a steady stream of receivers, we will be flying at their refueling airspeed of three-hundred, twenty-five knots and twenty-one thousand feet altitude according to your plan. At those conditions, we will go through our fuel quickly. But if we get our receivers in waves of aircraft, say six to eight at a time, we can go up to the top of our practice area in between waves, orbit at thirty-five thousand feet and slow down to holding airspeed. If we do that, we can make our fuel last much longer."

His pencil stopped. "Okay. Well, that is a lot of planning that we haven't done."

"Yes, sir. But there is more."

He laid the pencil across the pad. "What else?"

"Well, a KC-135 is a lot more fuel-efficient than your RF-4Cs. F-4s in general are notoriously bad on gas mileage. If we can make your guys wait until they are really low on fuel, and we can leave it in the KC-135 longer, we can offload it to them later in the mission. In that case, I think we can stretch out our time in the orbit and your airplanes' time on target by an hour or two. But that supposes that your guys are always in a position to get home if the tanker becomes unavailable for any reason. That's another thing that will take a bit of planning."

The commander was beginning to look flustered. "Can you, at least, estimate what time you will need to leave the practice area to go home?" he asked.

"Sir, think of it this way," I answered. "We are your asset. We will do everything we can to maximize our offload capability to your airplanes. But we are an asset that you can waste or use wisely. We will do our best, but when the fuel is gone, it's gone, and we must leave for home."

Then I smiled and let up on him a bit. "I would estimate from what I see looking over your pilots' shoulders and what they are planning that we can probably stay around three hours or so and offload forty to forty-five thousand pounds before we have to head out. There are other considerations, too. This all assumes that it does not rain tomorrow, it's not too hot, and that the tanker gets off the ground at all with that fuel load. And there are a million other little things, you know, but we will do our very best to be there for your exercise with lots of gas."

"Yeah," he said. At this point, he picked up his pencil and wrote "45K / 3:00" on his note pad, stood up, and said, "Okay, forty-five? That's less than I had hoped, but, well, okay. See you at the briefing."

I smiled to myself as he walked away, knowing that I could have gone 5,000 pounds either way based on the width of my pencil lead. While the performance of the KC-135A was less than we might have desired, the charts we used to determine what the airplane could or could not do were produced by thousands of hours of testing by Boeing and USAF test pilots. The graphs were exceedingly accurate and completely repeatable, having been proven and revised and polished over the years since the airplane was first flown. But the data was then reduced to a chart where the width of a pilot's pencil could easily account for 4,000 or 5,000 pounds of weight. Five thousand pounds of fuel was a lot for an RF-4, but it could be lost in a pencil line for us.

We did our best with what we had, but sometimes it seemed that we measured it with a micrometer, marked things with a crayon, cut it with an ax. Sometimes it simply was not possible to plan any more accurately with the tools we were given.

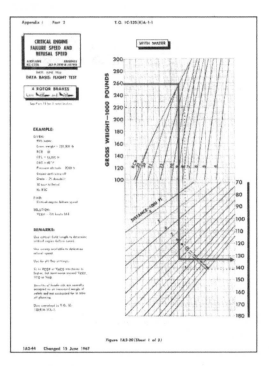

A takeoff planning chart from the KC-135A Flight Manual

Staff Sargent Frank Tesser was the boom operator for this flight, and he was seated about six feet behind Rick, with a great view of our instruments. The boom operator is the only enlisted person on the Steam Jet. Most of the booms will tell you that they are the only enlisted people anywhere who have three officers drive them to work! Their work, when they are not in the cockpit for takeoff and landing helping us, is to fly the refueling boom, make a safe contact with the receiver aircraft, and to act as our eyes and ears back at the refueling station which we all referred to as the boom pod. It was a job that took exceptional skill, and Frank was the best.

Bob Barrier sat right behind me by about three feet. At his navigator's table were all of the arcane instruments of his profession. He had at his disposal a Doppler Radar, a Weather Radar, and many tools we poor pilots could only guess at. But there were two things at his table that we all respected a great deal: his pencil and his brain. Why his pencil? Because it was the physical manifestation of his almost magical powers. Like all professional navigators, Bob worked from dusty old tables and graphs, instruments that taxed even his considerable abilities to describe. Using these, he produced magic: the magic of knowing where you were in the vast open oceans of the Earth and finding your way. It was a shame that Bob's job was being overcome by machinery, electronics, and automation.

I had seen navigators like him navigate all over the world, and I was never more impressed than on one occasion with our close friend, Captain Mark Stevens. Mark navigated from Phuket, Thailand to Diego Garcia, in the British Indian Ocean Territories (BIOT) located in the middle of the Indian Ocean. The journey covered 3,468 miles with no celestial fixes, no Doppler Radar, no Inertial Navigation System and, of course, no Global Positioning System (GPS). Mark's only functioning view of the world was through his ancient, black and white, airborne weather radar.

With just his radar and a pencil and some educated guesswork, for seven hours he saw no landmasses. We were over water, and there was not so much as a sand bar in this part of the Indian Ocean. For seven hours, Bob passed headings to fly around the thunderstorms that always seemed to be randomly dropped into the intertropical convergence zone around the Equator. The navigator would say on interphone to us up front, "Pilot, give me ten left," or "Pilot, give me twenty right on my mark ... now," or "Okay, twenty-three miles this direction, and we will need a forty-five-degree right turn."

By doing these calls and recording every turn in his notepad, he was performing a navigational method called "dead reckoning." At almost eight hours after his last fix from the land-based radio at Phuket, he said on the interphone, "Well guys, that's it. We are out of the area of thunderstorms, I see nothing, but clear ahead. Diego should be out there. If it is, we should know soon."

I turned for what seemed the hundredth time to look at him, face down in his notepad, checking his math again. Feeling not unlike Amelia Earhart and her navigator, Fred Noonan, looking for Howland Island, I look ahead and waited.

Diego Garcia is at the South end of the Chagos Archipelago in the middle of the Indian Ocean. It is so far from anywhere that the sailors, soldiers, and airmen that pass through claim that although it might not be the end of the world, you could see it from there.

As my view shifted back to the front, the number one needle on my VOR navigation radio receiver twitched for the first time in eight hours. As I watched, it rose to the very top of the case, pointing straight ahead. Mark Stevens had done the impossible by navigating a jet going 450 MPH with a pencil and a piece of paper.

He did not buy a beer anywhere I went ever again.

"Sir, it's the light in the number one handle," Frank said.

Rick and I both had short but acidic comments concerning the lineage of this particular airplane. When we were done insulting her, Rick sighed and settled into his seat for what he expected was going to be a long day.

"Okay, Nav. Can you talk to the tower and call the emergency for us? We are going to be busy for a bit."

Bob Barrier went to work.

"Bergstrom Tower, ROOK Seven Five declaring an Emergency, sir. We have a fire in our number one engine."

The color drained from Rick's face as he and I turned our attention to the actual fire light in the cockpit. Frank was right! A fire was indicated on our far left engine, known as the #1 engine. This was indicated by a single tiny light bulb that barely illuminated the poorly named "Fire Handle."

This was a very early version of a four-jet-engine airliner design, and there were some glaring differences between the KC-135A and a more modern commercial jetliner. The fire suppression system is a great example. The "Fire Handle" itself was only illuminated by a tiny bulb that we called a peanut bulb. There were no bells, or alarms, no "WARNING" or "CAUTION" lights, nor anything else to get the pilot's attention. The handle did not incorporate any fire extinguishers, so if we pulled it out during a fire, all that happened was that the fuel for the engine was shut off. Valves in the strut area between the engine and the wing were closed, stopping the flow of fuel, hydraulic fluid, electrics, and engine oil from the remote tank. Pulling the handle also shut off the hot, high pressure air from the engine, which *could* be the sole cause of a fire light on a good day. We were pondering the light, wondering if it was for real, when our KC-135A spoke for herself.

"BOOM!"

A loud explosion shook the airplane.

I looked down and noted the #1 engine instruments all racing for zero, and I called "Engine Failure!"

The aircraft lurched to the left and headed for the weeds and grass of the infield. While we were still accelerating on the runway, we were also well past "committed to takeoff" speed (S1). The time between passing S1 and achieving takeoff speed was one of the most vulnerable times during a flight. Our engine failure at this point was very dangerous.

Rick was a consummate Pilot (with a capital "P") that day. I heard him say the following mantra to himself: "Fly The Airplane." As Rick would tell me later, it was very sur-real after many years of flying airplanes, to look out the front windscreen and see grass! Without a word to anyone, Captain Packard **Flew The Airplane!**

Fly The Airplane. Three words are written over the main entrance doors of the Central Flight Instructor Course (CFIC) at Castle Air Force Base in Merced, California. Rick had been there. I had not, yet, but he told me what an influence those words had upon him. There are many dead pilots who forgot to fly the airplane. The CFIC instructor pilots felt that if there was one lesson that a prospective instructor pilot should take home with him from the central school, it was just that: so they had the words: "Fly The Airplane" written in large letters over the door of the school for all to see...and remember.

Rick pushed on the right rudder pedal, and he discovered that controlling an engine failure in the simulator was a lot easier than the real thing. He pushed in whatever it took, and he said later that it took all he could give. As we were already beyond our decision speed (S1), he steered the air-plane back onto the runway and waited for the airspeed to build. My job, as CP, was to support the AC, and simply sit in my seat and call out firmly and loudly whatever I might see that the pilot flying (Rick) might not already be aware of. I was supposed to be heard and support the Aircraft Commander by executing his commands. It was not my job to be liked or appreciated. If I had to take the airplane away from the pilot flying because he was not handling things correctly, it was my duty to do just that, immediately. Other than that, I did not say anything to the crew, and I did not touch anything by myself as I waited for Rick's command. I watched everything he did. And I never felt I could have done anything better than he did on that day.

The next thing I was supposed to do was to call out the airspeeds Rick needed to know. I had already called S1, and we were all waiting for the airspeed to reach Rotation Speed (Vr). Vr is the speed at which the flying pilot pulls back on the yoke and commits the airplane to flight. This is supposed to be done at the airspeed of Vr or when there is only 1,000 feet of usable runway remaining in front of the airplane, whichever occurs first.

As I watched the convergence of these two things, I soon knew that we would be about five knots too slow at 1,000 feet remaining.

"Thousand to go. Vr!" I yelled.

"Roger, Rotate," Rick said, and he began to pull.

There is a note in the KC-135 manual that says that a heavy KC-135 has about 2 degrees of pitch window at rotation speed. Too high, and the airplane will stall. Too low, and she will not fly. Rick hit the pitch exactly, and we cleared the runway with nothing to spare.

But our day was only beginning. When our Rate of Climb Indicator showed a positive number, Rick called "Positive Rate, Gear Up!"

I reached over and tried to raise the handle. Nothing. The handle wouldn't budge. I looked around to see if there was any explanation.

For a professional pilot at a moment such as this, there simply is no time to get frantic or scared. We couldn't afford that luxury at 165 knots and 100 feet of altitude over West Texas in a burning airplane. A pilot needs to be calm, deliberate, and timely in his actions.

Rick was holding a lot of right rudder to keep the airplane pointed straight, and because we were at a deficit for airspeed, he had to hold more than expected. Why? Because a slow airplane requires a more extreme input of control forces to produce the same result. More control input, because of the slower speed will, in turn, cause more drag. This slows the airplane even more. Unless something is changed, the pilot and his airplane will soon run out of airspeed and crash. It creates a deadly, vicious cycle. Dragging the landing gear around West Texas was a formula for a bad ending to our day. We really needed to retract it. Now.

Because the nose wheel follows the rudder pedals during takeoff, the nose wheel had continued to steer right, even though we had taken off and we were up in the air at that point. Normally, the nose wheel centered itself because it needed to be pointed straight ahead (centered) in order to retract normally. But because of the rudder input due to the failed engine, the nose wheel needed a little help from us.

It was not a fluke that Captain Rick Packard was considered the best pilot in the squadron. He was very bright; he was an IP and also a Check Airman. Imagine a career where someone could teach you a profession (instructor), but then, in order to practice your profession, you needed to be tested by a third pilot (the Check Airman). Rick also was the Crew Commander of S101, the most elite crew in the squadron.

Rick looked at the landing gear handle, which now had two, new, little red lights illuminated. One was in the small wheel at the end of the handle that told us that there was something wrong with the myriad interlocks that protected the landing gear on a normal day. The other was on the panel beside the handle. The single word below that light read "OVERRIDE."

Rick and I glanced at each other. We knew exactly what the other was thinking because we had spent the previous two years preparing for just this moment. We had studied the KC-135 manuals often on days when we were not flying, and we knew what to do in this particular situation and why. We would NOT override!

"Jiggle the nose wheel steering wheel," we both said. Rick Packard, while flying one of the most difficult maneuvers in aviation, reached down beside his left knee and shook the nose steering wheel. We heard a "clunk." The two red lights extinguished, and all of the landing gears retracted normally! The damaged KC-135A began to accelerate and climb.

Phew. Surely, we thought, now we were done?

All of this activity took place within about the first 30 seconds after we became airborne.

SPUR 13, one of the host unit's RF-4Cs was taking off behind us on that day, and I heard him call on the radio.

"ROOK 75, you have a fire in your number one engine!" He could not have known that Bob Barrier had already called the Air Traffic Control Tower on the other frequency.

At the time of his call to us, we were not allowed to talk on the radio. Our procedures for this type of emergency required us to AVIATE, NAVIGATE, and only then COMMUNICATE. We maintained cockpit discipline and watched as our aircraft struggled along, still moving slowly and not climbing very well because of our lack of engine thrust.

SPUR 13 had no way of knowing that, however. So, he switched his second radio to Air Traffic Control Tower frequency and said: "Tower, SPUR 13, I'm going to join ROOK 75 and check out his number one engine."

Not understanding why SPUR 13 would want to fly *toward* danger, the tower replied, "SPUR 13, break off the chase. The tanker has a problem."

At the point in time that so many might walk away, we breathed a sigh of relief. The pilot of SPUR 13 did not comply with the instructions from the control tower. He simply said, "Tower, SPUR 13. I'm going to join up with the tanker and check him out."

"Oh, okay," was the tower's response.

One of the items I was allowed to accomplish without hesitation in this sort of heavyweight emergency was to dump our excess fuel. We had taken off with over 95 thousand pounds of fuel. I was planning to dump it down to 70 thousand pounds. This would improve the performance of the airplane and make our landing roll shorter, too. It had taken me less than two seconds to start the process. The procedure was so simple it was a memory item for copilots. "Open-Close-Dump-Pump." Four switches. Two seconds. I was already doing that when Spur 13 appeared off our left wing and spoke up on our interplane frequency.

"ROOK 75. SPUR 13. You on?"

We had now been airborne about two minutes when SPUR 13 did a remarkable thing. He, essentially, took over the Air Traffic Control function. As a local pilot, familiar with the area, he saw that he was in a unique position to take over, and he assumed that responsibility. He may have even saved some lives that day, including ours.

"ROOK 75. SPUR 13. I recommend a right turn to heading 315. There's quite a bit of populated area to the north of the base."

Rick looked over at me, and with a head nod and a pointed finger, he told me exactly what I needed to do. I knew that he would talk to the chase airplane, and now was the time for me to coordinate with Bob, our navigator, to ensure all of the agencies that we were required to contact for our emergency had been contacted. Then I was to take over the ATC (Tower) communications, compute the landing data, post the numbers for him, run the engine failure checklist, the engine fire checklist, the fuel dumping checklist, the descent and approach checklist, and stop at the before landing checklist which we would all do together. This is the copilot's job.

Frank, our boom operator, had gone to the back of the airplane to look out our only window in the over-wing escape hatch. He reported back that he could not see the fire, but he did see us trailing a lot of black smoke ... and it was not getting better.

"Yeah, with winds calm, that's a pretty good idea," Rick said, referring to the 315 heading. "I'll maneuver south and get my ducks all lined up before I go in to land. I've got some performance considerations I've got to deal with before I go in."

"Performance? Oh, crap. That's me! Hurry up Bob. Make haste, carefully ..."

"How much time and gas do you have, and how many souls on board?" SPUR 13 asked.

"Six souls onboard and 80 thousand pounds of gas, headed for 70 at landing," Rick responded.

"How long before you're down to landing weight?"

"We'll be down to landing weight in a couple of minutes."

"Okay, reverse your turn and plan on a 35."

SPUR 13 was suggesting that we shorten the flight considerably as runway 35 was the same runway we had departed except that it was going back the other way. All we had to do was turn around. This maneuver really saved us a lot of time because we did not need to fly north of the field, endangering the City of Austin. Turning around like this also got us on the ground much more quickly. It was a pilot with local knowledge who was able to make quick decisions that aided us immensely in this emergency. I had a lot to do in that short time -- I had to work much faster than usual -- but our lives depended on me doing it all safely. I continued my work ...

"ROOK 75. SPUR13. The ILS to 35 is 110.3." I dialed the Instrument Landing System approach frequency for Runway 35 into the radio receivers as Rick continued to fly the airplane.

"Thanks. Okay, is that thing still smoking?" Rick asked.

"Yeah, well it's still aflame. It's not too much smoke, it's just sustained fire. It appears that it may be burning forward into the compressor section," SPUR 13 responded.

"Oh, no." Rick sounded even more concerned. "That's bad news. I've got to get myself on the ground. Quick."

"The field is at your 12 O'clock about 6 miles. You got it?"

"Yep. Thanks."

As we watched, SPUR 13 kept moving a little farther away from our left wing until he was about 200-300 feet away. We did not consider that a very high vote of confidence!

We finished all of the checklists about two miles out from landing, as we listened to SPUR 13 telling us we were still on fire. In fact, he said the fire was intensifying!

Rick looked at me, and I simply replied with a resigned sigh, "Landing Checklist Complete."

On a two-mile final, with a fire that was getting worse, Rick and I both knew we could not hurry. We had to fly the approach speed correctly, or the airplane might not be able to stop after landing. The last two miles were quiet on board our airplane as we flew toward the approaching runway and wondered if we were going to make it.

11

THE AIR MEDAL

The Air Medal

The crew of SPUR 13, the real heroes in my mind this day, could not land because we stopped our flaming airplane on the runway and closed the field while the fire department spent 20 minutes putting out the fire. They flew to San Antonio and returned later in the day.

Immediately after stopping, we jumped out of the airplane through the Crew Entry Hatch. This is the crew's normal way in and out of a KC-135. It is simply a vertical opening which comes up through the floor of the cockpit, immediately behind the AC and in front of the boom operator's position in the cockpit. There is a ladder to enter and exit as the floor of the KC-135 is ten feet off the ground.

As I went down the ladder, I might have hit a rung or two, but I don't think so. I went down feet first, but I only slowed my descent by my hands. As I reached the bottom of the ladder, the sound was the first thing I noticed. The fire was alive and breathing like a large dragon. It roared at me and made me feel very vulnerable. I felt my heartbeat and for the first time that day, I was scared. I really did not know if we were going to get away before it blew. I yelled up the hatch for everyone to hurry up and I counted them as they came down the ladder. When Rick came down, he yelled, "That's everybody!"

Just for a second, I turned and looked at the left wing. Because I had been sitting on the far side of the cockpit, I was the only one who had not seen the fire. The noise of the thing was unbelievable. I did not know that a fire could be that loud and sound so much like a living thing. It was huge and I realized *"wow, it's so damn hot!"* I could not see the number one engine. If it had fallen off, I would not have known it because the fire obscured everything beyond the number two engine.

Now the heat was starting to get bad and we needed to go. My thin NOMEX flight suit was no match for the flames 15 feet away. Two of the field's large firetrucks were pulling up and spraying their firefighting foam everywhere, and this was simply a very bad place to be right now. Rick and I turned and ran. We caught up with the other four members of our crew at our pre-designated place, which was 100 yards off the nose of the airplane. Again, we turned to look at ROOK 75 and we all felt the heat of the massive fire. We decided that we were still way too close. The second 100 yards was a lot easier to run.

The total duration of the flight, we only found out later, was just 12 minutes.

*   *   *

SPUR 13 and his squadron mates flew down to San Antonio, landed, refueled and waited. When they got the word that they could fly home, they were quickly airborne. As SPUR

13 taxied into his parking spot, a grateful crew of ROOK 75 presented both the pilot and his navigator with bottles of Jim Beam as Air Force tradition dictated.

Of course, the "Drinking of the Bourbon" was also an important part of the same Air Force tradition, so we all headed to the club to tell our stories and wait for our flying safety officer from Dyess to drive three or four hours down to see if we were okay. We knew, after all, that we were not going to be scheduled to fly for days, if not weeks, so a bit of alcohol seemed the order of the day!

We called our families and the 917th Air Refueling Squadron leadership to see if we should find our way home somehow or what. I mean, we couldn't fly that thing home, could we? At that point, we did not seriously even know if it would ever fly again. Our commander told us to just wait and see, and so we did. The flying safety officer had departed back to home base almost as soon as he had our blood and urine samples, and so we really were looking forward to an enforced vacation. Austin was fun.

The Number One Engine after the fire

Damaged Engine #1 cowling

Maintenance personnel arrived the next day and determined that the strut and the engine were totaled, but the attachment structure in the wing itself was okay. So, they put new electrical wiring and plumbing in what was left of the strut and hung a new engine on it. After hooking everything up, they towed it up to SAC Hill, where the Nuclear Alert Force at Bergstrom sat when this was a SAC base, and tried her out. The engine ran like a top! They placed a bit of silver tape on some of the holes in the strut and told us that we could fly the airplane but only low, slow, and straight home.

Austin to Abilene, Texas is only about 45 minutes in a KC-135A at low altitude and with just enough fuel to get there flying at 250 knots. Still, there was so much to do that day we did not land at Dyess until after 11:00 pm.

As we taxied into our spot at home, there was a crowd waiting to see the poor crippled airplane. They were disappointed. Except for the ugly tape all over the #1 strut, there was nothing to see. Our maintenance folks could not fly home with us. We had been restricted to "Essential Crew Only" for the ferry flight, so they had washed and scrubbed the soot off of the KC-135 and she looked pretty good. Nobody in Abilene had any idea how close we had come to a very different homecoming, and we agreed that was probably best. What they did not see was us inside the airplane, grinning and happy to finally be home.

What we could see, however, was the white top command vehicle of the Deputy Commander for Operations (DO) waiting for us to shut down our engines. As we did so, the car inched forward. Rick and I looked at each other.

"Think we're in trouble for something?"

I searched my mind to see if I could identify our error(s). This is what it was always like if you were a SAC aircrew member. There was even a faked up SAC Patch that said it all with only a hint of sarcasm: "To Err is Human. To Forgive is not SAC Policy!"

Finally, as we shut down our last engine and completed our parking checklist, we heard the Crew Entry Hatch open, and up came the DO. He did not say anything at all to us but simply turned right and went back to the pallet back in the cabin where we had brought back the burned cinder that had once been the number one engine of this airplane.

All we heard as he hastily left the flight deck was "Packard! Put your crew in for Air Medals." And with that, he was gone.

It was not SAC policy to create heroes, especially among the tanker crews, unless the commander had no choice. It turned out that the commander of the host unit at Bergstrom called our commander's commander and told him that if he did not put us up for medals, that he would take the unprecedented step of going across commands (TAC to SAC) and do it himself. The idea of that much fuel burning and trailing black smoke over Austin, Texas was his latest reason to lie awake at night, worrying. As far as I know, we were the only tanker crew to receive Air Medals since the war in Vietnam, and there were vanishingly few there.

Six weeks later, the Mishap Investigation Board (just like the one in which I had participated a few years earlier in Arizona) released their conclusions. In short, an internal fuel pipe that carried the fuel to the spray nozzles inside the engine had ruptured due to old age. The break quickly became a blowtorch and went through the side of our number one engine. The fact that the location of that hole, blowtorch included, just happened be at a critical junction of oil, hydraulic, and more fuel lines was just luck. In a quick explosion, all of those sources became involved and blew out a section of our outboard #1 cowling about the size of a dinner table. The fire was so hot that the famous "Boeing Firewall" that was supposed to hold any engine fires at bay for two hours, was compromised almost instantly and the fire was well into the strut as it burned up toward our Main Outboard fuel tank. How much longer we had to fly, no one could speculate.

We all agreed that we were lucky. Rick and I became long term friends on that day, much like brothers. We often tell people who ask about this, "Burning up an airplane together was kind of a bonding experience for us."

More than that, however, Rick Packard showed me how an aircraft commander should properly handle an emergency. Also, we received notoriety that we could have never gotten otherwise. Rick went on to stay in the Air Force and had a very successful career. He was chosen to fly the KC-10, the newest air refueling tanker in the world at the time, where he distinguished himself many times over. He achieved the rank of colonel (O-6), and retired after 26 years as the Commander of the Air Force Flight Safety Agency. Today, he lives in Sunderland, Maryland, with his wife Martha and he is still my very best friend and brother.

My notoriety turned out to be another "Big Hand." This time it helped me, which would not always be the case.

The Root Cause

Were we essentially, in the wrong place at the right time? Were we just lucky that day? Anybody could have done it, right?

Anybody, that is, if they studied as hard as we did. Anybody that had the support of others, like the crew of SPUR 13 who, themselves, had great courage and knew where and how to help and did so. Anybody with a bit of luck. Anybody who had the courage to sit there in a ticking time bomb, flying the proper approach speed when hurrying might well have killed everybody on board along with so many others in Austin, who were also lucky on that hot day in August 1982 and did not even know it.

12

THE GUCCI BOYS

KC-10 Promotional Cartoon Image

After the notoriety of the Air Medals we received for our emergency at Bergstrom AFB, I realized that I could use that as an introduction to other units that might be looking for a pilot. I did not have my three years at Dyess, yet. I was busy gaining additional flight experience in the old T-37 again from pilot training in addition flying to my regular schedule as a KC-135 copilot. The program that allowed me to get more experience was called Accelerated Copilot Enrichment (ACE). The people up at Headquarters SAC had noted that their copilots were not fully ready when their time came to upgrade to Aircraft Commander. So, they provided each SAC base with a few surplus T-37 or T-38s and encouraged their copilots to go fly them. Two copilots, one airplane, aeronautical decision-making education, at its best! At Dyess, where I was stationed, we received T-37s.

I would have LOVED to fly the supersonic T-38 instead of the T-37, but a free airplane with the chance to go anywhere in the continental United States anytime my schedule was open, and on my own time was great. All I needed was another copilot to go with me.

The ACE Program was there for one reason, to give copilots the opportunity to go out and learn from their own mistakes in a more relaxed environment than UPT. Sometimes I got to intervene in the other copilot's mistake to keep us both alive, but that experience is extra. The ACE program was strictly voluntary and it was considered an "additional duty" by my squadron. I saw it as a great opportunity. I just didn't know how much of an opportunity it truly was.

The ACE Program consisted of two or three Instructor Pilots from the nearest UPT base. Ours were from Laughlin AFB in Del Rio, Texas, and they had a T-shirt they awarded to the copilot who logged the most time in the T-37 every calendar month. I won that shirt almost every month.

Soon, my total aircraft time was over 1,000 hours and I was selected to upgrade to aircraft commander in the KC-135. I was sent back to Castle AFB in Merced, California to complete the training. I was the only lieutenant there for that purpose – everyone else was a captain. I completed upgrade to AC and returned to Dyess for the local familiarization flights that all new aircraft commanders receive.

When all of that was finished, I had to complete a solo flight as AC with my crew. I did not really fly the KC-135 solo, of course. During my first 100 hours after upgrade, I had to make all the takeoffs and landings myself. I was not allowed to let my copilot fly at all, so everyone *called it* a solo flight.

The date was May 10, 1983 -- my first solo in the KC-135. My crew and I refueled an E-3A Airborne Warning and Control System (AWACS) airplane. Returning to Dyess, the visibility and winds were perfect, but the realization the landing was strictly on me was somewhat intimidating. There was no one to whom I could say, "Could you land this thing. I am tired."

I only had one shot at the landing. NO touch and goes. Those were strictly for instructors. I flew an instrument approach that provided all the feedback that I could use to get me into the touchdown zone on the runway, and it worked like a champ. But then I needed to actually take over manually and land the plane (The KC-135 did not have "Autoland")

I was very aware that this was where most KC-135s are lost. About once per year, someone loses control of the KC-135 during landing and it can all go very badly in a big hurry. When I started to flare (pull back on the controls to soften the landing), I just did not feel confident in myself and the airplane was beginning to wobble a bit. My choices were to land anyway and take my chances or go around to try again even though I was aware of the people who were gathered around to watch and critique the new AC. They would all have something to say. Not nice stuff. I did not have any more time to make up my mind. I did the only thing I knew to get myself more time.

"Crew, we're going around," I said.

"Set power."

"Positive rate... Gear up."

In doing a go-around from about 5-10 feet off the ground, I broke a host of SAC rules. God bless my crew, however. They never batted an eyelash. They all did their jobs and earned their pay on that day.

Once I had my hands on the airplane, it felt good. It flew just fine. I only needed a moment to warm up to it. I asked for a visual pattern and we landed without incident.

As we taxied to the parking area, I could see three of the white topped command vehicles "escorting" me to the spot. I was busy parking the airplane, so when I looked up, they were all gone. No, wait a minute, there was one remaining, the DO. This was my colonel-boss who was so senior to me that I did not even want to think about it. Once again, I had that awful feeling when the 'old man' steps into the cockpit and just stands there waiting for the crew to finish their last checklist.

When we were done, he said, "Welcome back gentlemen. How did it go, Bob?"

"Well, sir, everything went fine except for that first approach. I just didn't feel comfortable about it, so I went around. We were well below 200 feet, and I know...."

"Good choice," he said. "Yeah, I saw that. You could have landed it, but you played it safe and smart. Good landing out of the visual, though. At least I don't have to worry about *your* judgement. Congratulations. You're done!"

After shaking hands all around, he headed for the boarding ladder. As he went, however, I could see that he was shaking his head and saying, "... first lieutenant. I'll be damned ..."

And that is the punch line: I was still a First Lieutenant. I was only the second person at Dyess since the Vietnam era to complete upgrade to AC as a lieutenant in the KC-135. I flew out the rest of my tour in KC-135s as a first lieutenant aircraft commander.

Rick Packard had already received an assignment to the 9th Air Refueling Squadron (9 ARS) at March AFB in Riverside, California as a KC-10 aircraft commander. The 9 ARS at March and the 32 ARS at Barksdale AFB, Louisiana were the only two places where the KC-10 Extender, the newest aircraft in the Air Force inventory, was just coming on board.

For SAC tanker pilots, this was the Holy Grail. Imagine going from an airplane that is as old as you are to an aircraft that is still being delivered from the factory! Trade in your old water injected, 287,000-pound Steam Jet for a brand new 590,000 pound whisper-jet! For any tanker pilot, this was THE dream assignment. Also, instead of going to the Alert Pad one week out of three and sitting and studying your airplane just to have something to do, the KC-10 had no alert commitment. These brand new, beautiful, white-topped planes were going places, developing new tactics, no longer restricted to SAC bases only (as it hauled cargo as well as acting as a refueler), and being the star of the show at air shows around the world.

KC-10 at an airshow

A KC-10 pilot assigned to March AFB, for example, could expect to spend about 150 days per year overseas in the Pacific and Far East. Places like Hawaii, Guam, Japan, the Philippines, South Korea or Diego Garcia were possible. If they found themselves assigned to Barksdale AFB, he or she could reasonably expect to spend a similar amount of time in England, Spain, the Middle East, Italy or any of the NATO countries, and more. It was hard to see any downside to it.

As I was approaching my three-year mark at Dyess AFB, it was mid-September of 1983. I was aware that I was approaching the assignments "witching hour." That was the time where an Air Force pilot needed to find a new assignment for him or/herself before the faceless people in the personnel office sent them to a place where they did not want to go. I had remained in contact with Captain Packard and I was convinced that I wanted an assignment to KC-10s, also. So, I called the number for the pilot assignments office and introduced myself. When I asked about getting a KC-10 assignment, something must have clicked in the brain of the person on the other end of the line because he asked, "Are you the same Hendrickson who got the Air Medal for that KC-135 fire in San Antonio?"

"Well, it was Bergstrom, but yeah. That's me."

"I just saw you in the Combat Crew Safety Magazine! That was cool," he said. "Just a minute ... uh, okay. You know they just had a selection board for new KC-10 pilots?"

"Oh," I said. I was disappointed. "No. I did not know that. What do I need to do to be considered next time?"

"Not a thing," he replied. "Let's see, you know it's a long list here. 175 tanker pilots met the board, and they only selected a handful." He mumbled a few things like that and in about a minute more, he asked "Okay. I need to start a new list here for notified, and ..." his voice trailed off. More shuffling of papers. "I need to notify the selectees. Today."

Listening to him fumbling around was excruciating. What was he doing?

Then he spoke up in a different tone of voice.

"How soon can you be there?"

"Oh! I made it? Wow! Great! Uh, be there? I don't know," I stammered. "Two, three weeks?"

"How about two? Your class would start on Monday, October 17th."

I had never seen, heard of, or experienced any assignment being passed out to anyone so quickly or so easily, especially a cherry assignment like a KC-10. I was just about to hang up, after thanking him profusely, when I asked, "Oh, I almost forgot. Where?"

"Barksdale."

Getting out of Dyess in two weeks was a bit of a challenge, but Joni and I were living on-base, so we did not need to sell a house. That was a bonus! At the time, Joni was not working, so we simply packed up and moved. We made the five-hour drive to Barksdale in our two separate cars two weeks later. I was smiling the whole way.

*   *   *

The Flight Scheduler in a flying squadron is one of the most important people in the unit. That's who determines when and where crewmembers fly, and that is everything! So, whenever a new arrival shows up at a unit, the pilot will usually stop in to see the scheduler as a very high priority. That way, the pilot knows when and where their next activity will be and who to talk to if there is a conflict. The Flight Scheduler has, by far, the largest office in the squadron building because one wall is usually occupied by a huge piece of Plexiglas upon which the scheduler has written activities in the form of some code words by everyone's name. If a pilot wants to go to the very best places and fly the most interesting missions, then he should get a cup of coffee and go down to the scheduler's office and ask him if he needs help. The pilot will soon lean why the scheduler's job has been compared to a Rubik's Cube. Everything touches everything else. To this day, whenever I have a recurring dream, it involves sitting around the scheduler's office and moving activities around in my schedule so I can volunteer for that next big trip for myself and my crew!

The very first thing I did when I arrived at my new KC-10 assignment at Barksdale was to walk into the squadron scheduler's office and stick out my hand and introduced myself.

"Hi. Bob Hendrickson. I saw one in the pattern." Meaning that I had seen a KC-10 practicing landings. "How many are flying today?"

'Hi Bob," he said, looking at the board. "That's a reserve crew in the pattern, with our newest KC-10, tail number 83-0075, and well, that's it. That's seven airframes."

"Wow!" I thought. *"7 out of 30. New ones coming. This is going to be fun!"*

As we made small talk, I looked at the "Big Board." There were numbers down the left side: 1 thru 50, but the column was mostly empty. But, beside the number 17 was my name: HENDRICKSON, R / CP. So, I was the 17th line pilot to fly the KC-10 at Barksdale. I knew that I wouldn't be getting the AC slot for some time. I was still a first lieutenant and I did not have enough command time to qualify, but that was okay. My foot was in-the-door. And only seven out of the eventual 30 airplanes were parked outside. I rubbed my palms together. This was like heaven! New unit, new planes, new places. What else could a pilot ask for?

The next day, I was sent down to get my flight and personal gear. In every flying unit, the new pilot is issued his flight gear. This ensures that every pilot starts with all his required flight suits, scarves, garment bags, travel gear, etc. Some of these things may vary from unit to unit and from airplane to airplane. For instance, in the 32 ARS, we were issued flight suits but no helmets (as in the KC-135). We were issued travel bags (luggage) and not G-suits (as in a fighter squadron). In other flying squadrons, you were issued gear from a pile of serviceable leftovers from the pilots who had departed the unit before you arrived. In a newly created KC-10 unit all the gear I was issued was brand new.

When we showed up on the flight line or in a briefing in all our freshly issued gear, we stood out from the other crews. Our stuff was clean and new. Our airplane was clean and new. Our tactics were new. We flew cargo as often as we performed air refueling. We did not sit on alert as our brothers and sisters did in the rest of Strategic Air Command. We were treated as something of an elite unit largely because of the airplane and its newness and because KC-10 aircrews were handpicked from the very best that SAC had to offer. It was inevitable that we would receive comments from those who were not chosen for this unique opportunity. Soon, other pilots were calling us the "Gucci Boys."

The origin of the term Gucci Boys has been attributed to the March AFB KC-10 units, but it was not long before all of us were being called Gucci Boys behind our backs. At first, I did not know how to deal with this name. It was not given in jest so much as a comment on our supposedly huge egos. They were saying, quite clearly, that we were just a bunch of prima donnas, that we were putting on airs.

This was the first time I had felt the rejection of a few malcontents who, like crabs in a bucket, would seek to pull any escapees back into the bucket rather than see anyone escape their fate. I was embarrassed by this at first, until I observed my fellow "Gucci Boys" who adopted the nickname and turned it around. After all, we *were* the special ones. We were all hand-picked for this job. We were the elite. And so, we were, indeed, "Gucci Boys!"

I felt extremely lucky. I found myself in the company of some of the most outstanding pilots that I have seen anywhere. They knew things about the airplane and the mission that only the "Initial Cadre," as they were called, could have known. The "Initial Cadre" were the pilots who for the past three to five years had defined the Advanced Tanker/Cargo Aircraft mission, chosen the DC-10-30 derivative that became the KC-10, deployed the airplanes, and introduced the new machine and all of its capabilities into the Air Force. They were, in fact, elite pilots and officers who had done a remarkable job bringing this airplane to the fight.

I was in the first group of pilots selected *after* the Initial Cadre. I was in a group of pilots who followed the elite team and we did our best to continue the remarkable job that they had done. I find now, looking back at the names, that the people in the 32nd were truly amazing in many ways.

We had one pilot, Pam Melroy (now a retired colonel), who became a test pilot and NASA astronaut and flew on three space shuttle flights and was the commander of Space Shuttle mission STS-120. Pam was recently named to NASA's Astronaut Hall of Fame (and, yes, I was jealous!). We also had a young pilot named Paul Selva who rose to the highest rank in the Air Force, a four-star general and Vice-Chairman of the Joint Chiefs of Staff. Those were just two of the great pilots and extraordinary individual officers who would go on to distinguish themselves in many amazing ways.

A KC-10 escorts 4 Navy A-7s somewhere over the Indian Ocean
Circa 1985

13

BOMB COMP

(L to R) Capt Mike Precht, TSgt Harold Norwood,
Me, and SSgt Scott Rhodes
Moments prior to our takeoff on the final flight in which we
won the 1986 SAC Bombing and Navigation Competition.

I drank it all up, and I progressed quickly. Rapid advancement was easier when the 32 ARS was growing so fast. By the summer of 1985, I was an aircraft commander in charge of my own crew when the squadron commander summoned me to his office.

"Hi Bob. Come in and sit down, please." He had the squadron's Operations Officer in the room also.

I thanked him and automatically began to wonder what I had done this time. As I sat, I knew that I should probably wait to speak until I knew what this was all about.

"So, Bob, you are back in command of the airplane. How do you like that?"

"I think it is great! I am flattered that the Air Force would place that kind of trust on my shoulders. I just hope I can live up to it."

"We have no doubt about that," he replied. "But we want you to fly some sorties back in the right seat for a bit because we have a special assignment for you."

Where is he going with this? I wondered. *I mean, I know that we do a lot of secret missions and a lot of Distinguished Visitor (DV) stuff, but what is this?*

He went on, "You will still fly as Aircraft Commander on your share of sorties, but we want you to fly as a Copilot for Captain Rick Spott, for the Bomb Comp."

BINGO!

The Strategic Air Command's Bombing and Navigation Competition (Bomb Comp) was the premier SAC flying competition at the time. Sometimes called the World Series of bombing and navigation, it pitted the best crews from each unit in SAC and often crews from our NATO Allies against one another to see who was the best at bombing (for the bombers), and navigation (for the tankers). One designated crew from each SAC squadron flew a few practice sorties against the radar scoring sites out in the western United States, and then flew two for the money. One of those two competition missions was flown at night, one was during the day.

The best scores on the maneuvers won the day, and the victors were named as the Best Crew in SAC (for their particular airplane). Their unit and the wing won the "Bomb Comp." Captain Derrick (Rick) Spott had just competed in the Bomb Comp the previous year as the CP, and his crew had been victorious. Now Rick was to be the Aircraft /Commander as well as an Instructor Pilot. (AC/IP) and they wanted me to fly as his Co-pilot.(CP). This was a solid vote of confidence in me from both my commander and my Operations Officer!

"Of course, I will. That would be wonderful," I quickly answered.

"Good! We did not know if being a copilot again would be a problem."

"Not if I'm flying with Rick Spott," I said.

Being a part of Bomb Comp was not my specific aim. My primary goal in this squadron was to be the one pilot my commanders would go to when a mission was particularly complex, dangerous, or difficult. If I were that "go-to" pilot, my number-one goal would be satisfied. They seemed to have chosen me for that role and I was secretly happy, but also scared. I knew that if I was in the spotlight, all my mistakes would be spotlighted, too.

"Well, great! Go have fun, but go win!"

"Yessir!" I stood, saluted, and made my exit.

We flew nine practice sorties for the 1985 competition, and then completed the two scored missions. On the night sortie, we made our turn inbound to our first target (we would be scored on four tasks that evening) and discovered that our forecast winds for the night were very wrong. The winds aloft were off by 150 knots! This is what we considered a "busted forecast" by our weathermen at Barksdale. We could not make it to the target on time, even if we flew at the airplane's maximum allowable airspeed. We flew as fast as the airplane would go, but we were still 20 seconds late and we knew we had lost. We felt that an error of 20 seconds at this level of competition would almost certainly doom our chances. Despite our misgivings about our performance on the night sortie, we attended the banquet where the winners were to be announced. We wondered how close we had come to whoever was the winner. When the winners of the 1985 Best Crew in SAC were named, they read our names! We had won! At 20 seconds off target, we still were closer than anyone else that night. Why? I may never know. Maybe we all got the same forecast.

Much celebration followed, although I really do not remember much of it. What I did remember of the evening was the squadron commander telling/asking me if I planned to stick around and fly next year's Bomb Comp – this time as the Aircraft Commander. Of course I did.

During the next year, I flew my share of training and operational missions, including deployments to the Middle East (Saudi Arabia) as part of our ongoing support of that country's air defense. I also was chosen to upgrade to KC-10 instructor pilot and completed my training a few months before the 1986 competition. I flew the 1986 Bomb Comp for the 32 ARS, but I also acted as the project lead for all KC-10 units assigned to Barksdale AFB, the 78 ARS belonging to the Air Force Reserve (who were a separate entry in the competition). That meant I would spend the year identifying the most reliable and most accurate KC-10 aircraft for use by both squadrons.

My crew was selected for me by the squadron staff. They were chosen for their intelligence, skills, and their positive attitudes. Not that I ever had difficulty motivating any crewmember, ever, but these three were different. Each of them pushed me to give them more responsibility. Each of them truly loved what they did. I do not think I could have chosen a better crew for the 1986 competition.

My copilot was Captain Mike Precht. He was young. An experienced Copilot, he had not upgraded to Aircraft Commander yet, unlike my situation when I competed the year before. He was a great copilot, and so smart! Mike operated one of the calculators in the cockpit and assisted me in flying the airplane when needed.

The flight engineer was Staff Sergeant Harold Norwood. I had complete trust in Harold and he never let any of us down. He backed up the boom operator and was responsible for keeping track of all the aircraft systems while the rest of us puzzled out some new thing.

The boom operator was Staff Sergeant Scott Rhodes. Scott never refueled anyone during our Bomb Comp sorties, but he was busy, nonetheless. He was the other person in the cockpit, besides the Copilot and me, who used our secret weapon: the state-of-the-art Hewlett-Packard programmable calculator that we had programmed ourselves. With this calculator, we were able to fly orbits and other difficult maneuvers with relative ease because the calculator was programmed to provide us with detailed headings, airspeeds, and timing that the basic Inertial Navigation System did not provide.

We were able to do these things only because Scott was there, leaning over my right shoulder and saying "On time, 30 seconds to go, airspeed should be 327 knots. One degree right. Good. Good. On speed. Good. Five, Four, Three, Two, One, Hack!" After a few practice sorties, we developed our skills at this exercise so that we never saw any deviation from our recorded position and our desired position at time zero. Ever.

We were all pretty confident going into the banquet this time. We knew we had done our best, and that the competition would be chasing us. Barring any last-minute glitches, we felt cautiously optimistic. Because the 32nd had won the two previous competitions, it would have looked very bad if we had not won. We took the competition seriously, but we knew we had done well.

We won again! It was the third time in a row for the 32nd and two in a row for me.

Here I am holding the
McDonnell-Douglas KC-10 Trophy in 1986
It was renamed the General Ellis Trophy
for best KC-10 crew in SAC soon after

Rick Spott, the Aircraft Commander of our 1985 Bomb Comp crew, did not attend the banquet in 1986. In the year that had passed since the 1985 competition, he decided to take advantage of the opportunity available to serve his family better by becoming a pilot for the airlines. As his official date of separation was approaching, he was interviewing with some of the major carriers.

During his mini-physical interview at American Airlines, one of the doctors monitoring the testing called him over.

"What is your name, sir?'

"Derrick B. Spott." He replied.

"Mr. Spott. Did you know that you were walking funny? Did you hurt yourself in some way?"

"Not that I know of," Rick said. "I didn't know I was walking funny."

"Well, it's probably nothing, but you need to go get it checked out." The doctor advised. "Come back when you have done that." He handed Rick his application back.

Soon thereafter, Rick was diagnosed with Amyotrophic Lateral Sclerosis (ALS), also known as Lou Gehrig's Disease. His prognosis was in terms of how long he would live, not if he would ever recover.

I was devastated. I had always looked up to Rick and tried to be as good and genuine as he was. I was not alone. Our entire squadron was caught completely off guard. One of their very finest pilots, an exemplary officer, a mentor, a young husband (32 years old), and a father to two little girls was suddenly targeted by this terrible, virtually always fatal disease.

When he died, eighteen short months later, I was shattered. A very close friend, mentor, and all-round decent human being was taken from me and everyone who knew him in a slow and terrible death. There was a hole in my heart and in my life. It was not fair. Everybody who knew Rick knew that, too. It was just not fair.

I have lost loved ones and friends from my life, but Rick Spott's life was a target for me to strive for in hopes that I might achieve a small measure of his sincerity, leadership, and capacity for love of his family and friends. As much as I tried, I do not think I ever got close to his example except in one way, but that is another story that I will get to in a later chapter..

One day in September 1986, I was hanging around at the squadron, reviewing some all-important Officer Evaluation Reports (OERs). I had been chosen for that additional duty (OER Monitor) because my commanders thought I could write – at least they thought I was better than most of the math and engineering majors in the 32 ARS. I had recently completed KC-10 instructor training and I was looking forward to having a hand in training the next batch of pilots coming into the squadron. Approaching three years in the unit, I had logged well over 2,000 hours in the airplane and traveled all over the world. I was ready for more.

Bring it on! I thought.

14

JONI

My marriage to Joni had never been anything to brag about. What might have been the tree we had planted (metaphorically representing our love) had never taken root and had died not long after our 1974 marriage. She had her friends and I had mine and she rarely came to anything social involving the Air Force. When she was compelled to attend some of those events anyway, she was insufferable to everyone. She was happy to tell anyone around her that she was a "bitch," and she had the T-shirt to prove it (and she did). I was just suffering along with the situation because breaking up with her seemed to me to be more difficult than leaving well enough alone. The truth is I had never recovered emotionally from my breakup with Kip many years before.

I had never seen, heard of, or known of any relationship like the one I had with Kip. I reasoned that I could leave Joni, but then what? We had been together for more than 13 years at that point and my emotions had become cauterized by the negative heat and flames emanating from my wife. If I sent her away, I would be truly alone. Somewhere, over the past 13 years, I had come to realize that I was afraid to be alone. So, I was living in this limbo that I never really carefully thought through.

As I sat at the government-issue desk in the squadron, looking over someone's OER, newly minted Captain Paul Selva strolled into the room and announced, "They are looking for a KC-10 IP to go to Zaragoza, Spain for three years."

And then, as if he had not seen me sitting there, he turned to me and asked, "Hey, Bob. You're an IP. You want to go to Spain?"

He told people later that I had to think about his offer for three seconds before I could answer, but I beg to differ. I was a KC-10 Pilot. I only took two seconds!

"You bet! Where do I sign up?"

I felt that this was a real opportunity to do something new and exciting. It was different from the regular, normal, mundane life of a squadron-level tanker pilot who follows the sacred path to rank, leadership, and power, where the real cream rises to the top. I did not feel motivated by that. I felt I needed a break in my life. Maybe I could find another sacred path to my own holy grail in Spain.

Besides, I thought. *This sounds like an adventure! Isn't that what got me here in the first place?*

"I'm in!" I shouted.

This kind of decision-making was my trademark for much of my life. A search for thrills and adventure was the flavor-of-the-day. I did not know, at the time, why I sought these things. I just did. Maybe I had already done so many things in my life that were thrilling and exciting, it just took more to burn through the scar tissue to the place inside where I was forced to live with my worst critic: myself.

This time my permanent change of station (PCS) orders gave me a comparatively relaxing three weeks to pack up everything, sell the house and go overseas. I made the TWA 747 flight to Madrid with hours to spare!

Once Joni and I arrived in Spain and moved to the air base at Zaragoza, she and I were arguing again. My marriage to her finally ran out of whatever it was that had kept it going. Joni was extra miserable to everybody in Zaragoza, no matter if they spoke Spanish or English. I finally had enough, so with divorce papers in her hand, she went back to her hometown of Midland, Texas and I stayed in Zaragoza.

As divorces go, it was easy. I told her to take her stuff and leave mine. I think we disagreed who owned the painting over the fireplace, but except for that, 14 years split up easily. I am fairly sure the main reason it was easy was because we never really felt married to each other in the first place.

I called her a few days after she had returned to Midland, Texas to see how things were going.

"Hey, how was your flight?" I asked.

"It was okay. Long, but okay."

She went on, "I don't think I am going to be able to stand this West Texas heat very long. How long do you think it will be before we can get back together?"

Tears welled up in my eyes, because, after all the pain I had been through in the past, this was still a woman I had spent the last 14 years with. I still felt a connection.

"Joni, it's over. There will be no getting back together this time. I've made that clear."

She snorted derisively on the other end of the phone. "Well, I'm glad you called, anyway."

"Really?" I asked.

"You might want to get yourself checked out," she said defiantly.

"Why?"

"Doctor says I have Chlamydia!" She was positively laughing now. "You probably gave it to me from all the women you've been screwing!"

"Goodbye, Joni."

"Yeah. See 'ya later, prick."

Then she hung up.

I may never know whether she really had that disease. I do know this, I never did.

15

SOF

The KC-10 "Extender" – the
Air Force's Advanced Tanker/Cargo Aircraft

I was shivering and the night was as inky black as I had ever experienced. The temperature was a little cool at 19 degrees Celsius. I did a quick mental conversion, so my American mind could think. "Ah, 66 degrees. Not bad."

It didn't work.

The wind was right down the runway at about 12 knots. Again, not bad, but I shivered anyway.

I was shivering because I was outside at midnight. The darkness brings out all kinds of apparitions. Sometimes,

109

they are vague feelings, like raw fear. Sometimes they are fully formed. An old friend, a loved one. In our evolution, we were all just small mammals that came down from the trees, alone, armed only with a brain. Fear kept us alive. So, it stands to reason that this small animal is still inside each of us. It does not like to be outside, in the open spaces, in the dark, with no place to run and hide. That little guy feels very vulnerable out there exposed. With no safe place, he cannot avoid the unseen predator that will come out of the darkness, with teeth flashing, to violently tear him into small, bloody bites. It is visceral. It goes back to instinctive feelings we cannot un-feel. In prehistoric times, this instinct protected that little human mammal inside of us. Now, it is just an appendage, like its namesake, the appendix. Darkness is scary, but oddly, it is also thrilling.

I checked my watch. It was 2357 hours (11:57 pm); 8,132 feet away to my east, the brilliant lights of the first KC-10, the leader of a three-ship formation of KC-10s, were pointing at me. From over a mile and a half away, they were bright to look at, but they did not make a dent in the darkness of my surroundings at the end of Taxiway Bravo at Zaragoza Air Base in Spain.

The radio in my Supervisor of Flying (SOF) vehicle crackled to life.

"TEXACO one one heavy flight, Zaragoza Tower. Wind three zero zero at one two, Cleared for takeoff at your discretion. Time now two three five eight and zero seconds. Have a good one, guys."

"TEXACO one one heavy flight, roger. Cleared to go our discretion. See you in a few."

Then, silence again, and waiting. I leaned into the driver's side window of my brown pickup truck with the huge "SOF" painted on it, picked up the microphone and said, "SOF is in position." The reply was simply "Roger, SOF."

Performing as the Supervisor of Flying was my duty tonight. It was a duty I particularly enjoyed because it appealed to my sense of self–direction and I liked the feeling that I was alone out there. Any decisions I had to make were mine. It was as if I had a great sword. I could wield it or fall on it.

By regulation, the Supervisor of Flying at Zaragoza had to be a fully current and qualified instructor pilot assigned to one of the attached flying squadrons. The SOF was responsible for all things to do with airplanes on the field, 24 hours a day.

For me, this meant that for the duration of my 24-hour shift, I would ride around in my SOF vehicle, checking in on the maintenance status, operational readiness, and availability of all of the aircraft on the field to determine if the assigned missions would be possible that day and determine if I needed to take any action necessary to accomplish the mission. As SOF, I operated with the full authority of the Deputy Commander for Operations. I would need to be present at crew arrival at the aircraft and all the way through the engine start, taxi, and launch.

Just prior to takeoff, I would perform a mandatory "Last Chance Inspection" of the aircraft, checking for configuration, leaks, doors, lights, or anything else I could see from my vehicle. Then, if everything was in order, I would radio to the crew that they were cleared to go. If anything needed to be checked on, delivered, or dealt with, it was also my job to do it. When the airplanes returned from their missions, I would be waiting, sitting in my SOF vehicle, observing all landings, touch-and-go landing and takeoffs, low approaches, taxi operations, parking, crew transport, and debriefs.

My friend, Captain Steve Mitchell, in the
34th Strategic Squadron's SOF vehicle at Zaragoza

It is a huge, seemingly impossible job. It can be over-whelming at most large, busy air bases. At Zaragoza, however, it was fun. I loved it.

It was 0000 hours. Midnight. Takeoff time for the flight of three KC-10 tankers. As I watched, the lead tanker was already on the runway and turned the rest of his landing lights on. A moment later, I heard the huge tanker's three engines spooling up for takeoff.

I had exaggerated a little bit when I called "SOF is in position." Normally, being in position means that I am clear of their airplane and the crew of the big 590,000-pound airplanes. By announcing this, it meant they did not need to worry about me being behind one of their engines or in front of a wheel or some other place where they could inadvertently kill me with the push of a throttle. It was a courtesy call to tell them I was clear after their last chance inspection, and I was "in position" to observe their takeoff, from the start of takeoff roll.

That night, however, I was waiting in a position about 100 feet from the left side of Runway 30 Left at a point about

8,132 feet down the runway from where they would each begin their takeoff runs.

I knew that it would take little over a minute for the aircraft to cover the distance to me, so I had plenty of time to get out of my truck and sit on its hood. Since the wingspan of the KC-10 is 164 feet, that would put me well outside of the wingtip as they passed. And since I had done the takeoff computations earlier in the day with all the performance parameters figured in, I knew this would be their lift-off point.

As the first KC-10 headed my way, the little mammal inside of me was not happy.

Thrills are one thing, Bob, but this? Have you ever been this close to a 590,000-pound, fire-breathing, monster going past you at 193 miles per hour at the moment when it lifts off from the ground? What kind of turbulence does that produce? Can you stand up to it? What is the noise going to be like? Are you going to get in trouble? Blah, blah, blah ....

I swallowed hard. And I waited.

As I sat there, I watched the airplane coming. The noise was building so that it almost blocked out the sound of my heart.

Even now, as he was about 2,500 feet from me, I could have easily read a book by the landing lights, and they were still a half-mile away. That was when I began to worry that the crew might see me out here as they went by and wonder why I was there. It was safe, but unusual. *It was too late now*, I thought, so I simply sat there.

As the tanker got to about 1,000 feet from me, I could see the nose wheel begin to lift into the air. This was going to work out perfectly, I thought, and at 193 miles per hour, it was going to be quick.

By this time, the lights were blinding, the noise was a physical force that crackled and roared and very quickly, the light was gone, and the turbulence generated by the aircraft hit me.

To be honest, I thought it would be worse, but it was not so bad. It was about hurricane force. Not really so bad at all!

I looked at the departing aircraft now and saw, for the first time, the plume of fire coming from each of the three engines. At a normal, takeoff thrust setting, the fire ring is almost invisible, but at maximum thrust, at midnight, it was mesmerizing.

"Wow, you were right," a voice from beside me said. "Impressive! But only a buffoon would be any closer than this. That's intense!"

I turned to the source of the comment, and there was Rick Packard, sitting next to me on the SOF vehicle.

"Yeah, I guess, but don't you think it would be fun to be closer?"

"Fun? You have got to be kidding! A little crosswind, a heavy hand by the pilot, or engine failure – you know about engine failures, don't you?"

"I mean just the slightest glitch, whatever, and you'd be toast! Worse yet, what do you think might happen to the crew do if they hit 180 pounds of YOU out there? I know that would be no great loss to you," he smiled mischievously, "but they might have somewhere to go after all of this."

He was right, of course, and I quickly realized that the danger it would pose to the innocent crew was the biggest risk and it was the only argument that mattered to me. The risk to me really did not enter into the argument for me. To this day, I never came closer to the runway during takeoff than this one night in Spain sitting on the hood of the SOF vehicle 100 feet behind the hold line.

When the third plane went by, I got back in the SOF vehicle, put it in gear, made the U-turn and drove alone, in silence, back to the squadron.

Often, my conscience spoke to me, and sometimes it took on forms of people I knew, especially on dark nights. This time it was my old friend Rick Packard and the message from within was clear: Sometimes the thrill of something is not worth the risk required to get that thrill. I knew that already, of course, but what I never considered before was that the risk might not be the risk to me, but it could be the risk to others because of my actions.

Maybe I was starting to grow up and understand that risking my own life for a thrill impacted others in ways that were hard to quantify.

"SOF is clear," I said into the radio.

"Roger, SOF. Good-night."

16

THE GREATEST THRILL OF ALL

Karen Landers Hendrickson

"Think not you can direct the course of love,
for love, if it finds you worthy, directs your course."

– Kahlil Gibran

The tires of the VW Vanagon barely had time to squeal before the impact. I was driving Karen's van back to her apartment in Concord, NH. My flight to Boston Logan Airport had been uneventful but the two-hour drive north on I-93 to Concord was not an example of my best day at driving. Karen had come down to Logan to pick me up. She was dressed in an L.L. Bean ski-sweater that had little reindeer all around the bodice. She had on a pair of petit-size jeans and white sneakers that were just the right mix of informal "I don't give a flip" and "Look at me!"

It was the same devil-may-care look that had me captivated, feeling lucky indeed, just to be with her. For the second time in my life, I was lost to the eyes of a woman. This time it was Karen, with her dark hair, fabulous smile, athletic build, and those stupid plastic sunglasses that she had spent way too much for. I gave her a good-natured razzing about those sunglasses, and she was laughing and calling me a name. I could not look at anything else! I should have ....

I was back in the United States from Spain for my quarterly refresher KC-10 simulator training. I was required to fly back once every quarter to attend these training sessions, and every six months, they would include a check ride for me, too. When it became apparent that I would finish the refresher training on-time, I called Karen in Concord to ask if she had the time for a short visit from me as I was passing through New England. She said that sounded like fun and so we set the "date." This date, however, got very interesting, very fast.

As I jammed the brake pedal to the floor, I knew I was not going to be able to miss him. I had been going a little under the speed limit, but I had been looking at Karen, my brunette vixen in the passenger seat. My thoughts were scattered, and I had not had an instant to get them corralled.

Why was this car stopped in the fast lane of a 65-mph freeway?

There were about three other cars on the freeway, one of them right beside me so I could not go around the parked car.

Am I going to die? Is Karen going to be all right?

Man, she is beautiful over there on the passenger side, turned around in her seat facing me. How does she do that?

Will I be in trouble back at Zaragoza, when they find out I am here, with her? Man-o-man, she is beautiful.

Wait a minute! Is that car backing up? Shit!

In the Fall of 1988, I was still the only KC-10 pilot assigned to any overseas location, but the nature of military assignments at that time guaranteed that I could not stay in

117

Zaragoza very much longer. I was either going to stay in the service or separate from the Air Force next October and I needed to decide. I had already been "volun-told" that if I remained in, I would be expected to serve three to six years at a desk in the Pentagon or Headquarters SAC.

That did not appeal to me at all, especially since my prior service made me older than my peers and I just wanted to fly. Looking beyond the headquarters assignment, I would be expected to assume command of some flying unit, somewhere, and the idea that I would be responsible for a lot of people did not appeal to me, either.

I had seen commanders who received praise for their unit's good work. I had also seen other commanders who seemed equally competent skewered by their superiors over matters that were absolutely out of their control. I had that happen to me once, back in Barksdale.

My assigned copilot had received a DUI from the base Security Police. I had been out of town on Temporary Duty (TDY) flying a KC-10 mission when I got the word. When I returned to Barksdale, I was summoned directly to the squadron operations officer's office.

"You know, Bob, while you were out instructing Lieutenant So-and-so on Friday night, I had to go down to the brig and sign out your copilot. Man, he was stinko! And he got a DUI out of it. What's going on?"

"Well, sir," I began. "I haven't seen him for about a week, and when I do, I will get his side of it. I will let you know, immediately!"

"Listen, Captain Hendrickson," he continued. "Being a crew commander makes you responsible for your crew's actions, whether you are here or not. Is that clear?"

"Yes, sir!" I stood up, executed my very best salute, and waited.

He looked at me, and from that moment, I knew he was in a box just like I was. How do you control the unseen?

"Dismissed," he said.

For a moment, I actually felt sorry for him.

I have heard it said that it only takes one "Cold Prickly" to equal a hundred "Warm Fuzzies." This was the same man who asked me to fly the Bomb Comp and so many other important missions. I had flown all over the world with him, shared countless dinners and box lunches, and yet I knew that my OER was sitting on his desk and he would be expected to take a bit of my hide when he completed it, or he could expect to get a bit of his own hide lifted when his OER became due.

Every pilot who had flown in the Bomb Comp before received an endorsement on his OER from the three-star general in his chain of command. A three-star endorsement was a sure-fire way to be in line for a coveted below-the-zone promotion to major. I was the only exception to that rule at the 32nd. My endorsement did not even leave Barksdale – it was only from a one-star general. I felt like I had returned to the searing disappointment I felt at being awarded a support type aircraft instead of a fighter during Assignments Night in Undergraduate Pilot Training back in 1980. Knowing why I had lost again did not lessen the sting.

I was required to remain current in the KC-10, but I realized I also needed to have some backup plan. I needed to get my Airline Transport Pilot (ATP) license so I could begin interviewing for an airline job. I needed to work on this because of the long lead-times, but I really did not have to make the final decision for months yet. As it happened, that decision was made for me.

Karen was the most radiant, beautiful woman I could ever remember seeing. She had been married when I first become aware of her in Zaragoza, Spain, so she was "off limits" to me, officially. But by the time I saw her in New England that day, she had left her husband and divorced him. Now she was living in Concord, NH. She had departed Zaragoza even before their divorce was final, so there was not even a chance for any sparks between us in Zaragoza, but I could not get her smile out of my mind, and I was single, too.

I was not even doing the 65-mph speed limit and that probably saved us. When I hit the brakes, she screamed and slipped into the foot well of the Vanagon in front of the passenger seat.

Just as I concluded that we were definitely going to hit that other car, the other driver glanced in her rearview mirror and hit the gas. It was too little, too late. I still hit her car, but thankfully, the difference in our speeds was not as great as it might have been otherwise.

Poor license plate! When we hit the other car, the numerals on Karen's front plate were flattened. But that was it. Karen was uninjured. None of us had a need for ambulance or police assistance as we got off at the next exit and exchanged information. As we drove home, I was thankful for Karen's escape, thankful for only light damage to the Vanagon, and thankful that I did not need to go back to Spain having to explain some stupid auto accident. The gossip was already fever-pitch back there because there was a rash of marital infidelities to talk about on the small, American air base at Zaragoza.

We had heard the gossip around the air base for months. Her marriage and mine were the fodder for many wagging tongues. Both matrimonial unions had been removed from life support and the divorce papers had been signed. The shipping containers for Karen and her kids (Whitney, Andrea, and Kyle) had been picked up at her house in La Muela, Spain to make the big move back to the states. Karen left Spain in the Spring of 1987 and set herself and her three children up in a two-bedroom apartment in Concord. Her divorce became final in October 1988.

After Thanksgiving of 1988, I went to my quarterly refresher simulator training at Seymour Johnson AFB in North Carolina. Afterwards, I flew to Boston Logan Airport.

Karen met me there, and I enjoyed a very nice, albeit short, visit with Karen and her kids. Afterward, I flew back to Spain.

The freeway accident made me realize two things. The first thing was that if I wanted to pursue a relationship with Karen, I was going to have to get out of the Air Force. A relationship with her would end my career, regardless of the fact that she was a single divorcee. Because I met her when we were both married to other people, there were always going to be those who would think the worst. The second thing I realized was that I didn't care. I loved the Air Force and I really loved my job and the KC-10 but I was *in* love with her. She just didn't know it yet.

So, when I arrived back in Spain, I went to speak to her ex-husband who worked on base. I told him flat out that I stopped in Concord and had seen Karen on my way back on this trip. I told him that she had been a perfect lady and that I wanted to see her again.

It wasn't that I wanted his permission, I just wanted him to hear it from me first, and not from the gossips down on the base. I thought that by treating this delicate subject with integrity, honesty, and candor, he might see that I was sincere.

Man, was I wrong!

"Oh my God!" he said. "So that's why she left me. She was in bed with you!"

"No, that's not true," I countered. "She was a married woman with three children while she was here. She would never be doing such a thing with me or anybody else. She is too good for that, and you know it!"

"Yeah, well. But were you 'attracted' to her while she was here?"

"Hell, I don't know. Maybe." Things were going off-the-rails quickly. "But I swear to you, nothing happened here."

"Yeah, yeah," he said. "But you were attracted to her."

Then he left.

121

At least, I had been honest with him. I felt bad, but I knew that what I was doing was legal and moral. I also knew that when the gossips down on base found out, all hell would break loose because the story would be juicy. I was a bit surprised when the news (at least *his* version of it) hit the base in about 30 minutes – the time it took him to drive there.

From the moment (plus 30 minutes) that I opened my mouth to him, I was a pariah on base at Zaragoza for the next year and a half. I lost most of my friends and my career in the Air Force would soon be over. As I had predicted, my commanders made it clear that if I had wished to remain in the Air Force beyond my scheduled date of separation, the price would have been unthinkable.

It was a very difficult time for me. I was alone in Spain, a social outcast, longing for the touch of a woman who was so very far away and counting the days until I could get on with my life.

On October 6, 1989, I separated from the Air Force to begin training at Trans World Airlines (TWA) at John F. Kennedy Airport as an international flight engineer on the Boeing 747. I moved to New York City and continued my long-distance courtship of Karen whenever I could.

One of the scariest crossings I ever attempted was making the crossing to what was an entirely new place for me. This crossing took 30 years to materialize. To put this in context, I was 36 years old when I met Karen. I was very, very single, and childless. At the time I thought I wanted it that way. But I was head over heels for her, and I told her so. One day as we were riding in the car, she turned to me and spoke up.

"Remember, I'm a package deal. I come with three kids: 4, 6, and 8. If you want to marry me, you have to marry them, too."

She wanted me to be a father!

I did not take her caution lightly. I knew it was true; however, I had never so much as changed a diaper, nor even held a baby in my arms. I was an absolute novice as I sat for weeks and contemplated what I could do about wanting Karen, but not knowing one way or the other what it was like to be a father to three precocious children.

Also, I was scared. Nobody had talked to me about how to do this parenting part without any training. It never occurred to me that every parent I ever knew started with exactly the same child-rearing experience I had. Zero.

So, this crossing was different from the normal crossings I experienced. It was not about training. I had the same people to help me in an ocean crossing as anyone else had in a similar position. Yet, in the situation I was now facing, I could look forward to the help of a loving wife. This time was different, though. This time it was strictly about me finding the courage to take the leap.

*   *   *

Sunday, January 7, 2000.
Walking back from the store in Concord, NH

Karen and I had walked to the grocery store to pick up a few items for us and her children for the week. The kids had quickly grown to accept me. It was easy enough. They had known me in Spain, and I was already familiar to them. Whitney and Andrea were quick to accept me, as their relationship with their father had never amounted to anything. With Kyle, it was different. Not only was he the youngest and he found difficulty in switching allegiances, but his father had doted on him as he did not on the girls. I suppose he felt that the boy was better suited to carrying on his "legacy" in a way that his girls could not. I thought he would miss the girls later. Karen had just started nursing school, and I was between assignments at my new airline job with TWA.

Like many airlines in 1990, TWA had a "B scale" for newly hired pilots like me. At TWA, the much lower B pay scale ran for five years before the "new hire" was eligible for normal pay. The B scale amounted to a fraction of the contract pay scale and it was supposed to help the airlines through rough times. To make ends meet, I lived in a house in Valley Stream, New York, with 11 other new hires. We called it our "crash pad." We were not alone. There were hundreds of crash pads around the nation's airports occupied by new hires.

It might have been fun except that a new-hire pilot on the B scale with a small family easily qualified for food stamps. The poverty endured by B-scalers was epic and common. Hot sheet crash pads (meaning that two or more pilots might share a bed on alternate nights, but they would change the sheets on arrival) were the norm, and sometimes, B-scalers were seen sleeping in recliners or on couches in the terminals and hangars around the airports. I stayed in TWA's Terminal Five at JFK Airport many hundreds of nights while sitting on reserve.

As Karen and I walked back from the store, we were talking.

"Wow," I wondered. "I just can't believe how much food costs back here in the U.S. At least I have next week off, so I don't have to eat out in New York or Europe. You know how hard it is to keep anything in a fridge in a crash pad when you're one of ten people living there and you're only there three or four times a month for an overnight. Eating out in Paris, now that is expensive!"

"Oh, give me a break," she laughed. "How many of your friends at the other airlines would love to have the problem of how to spend their per-diem on dinner in Paris?"

"Well, yeah," I replied. "But their per-diem is twice what mine is. Think how nice it would be if I could bring some of that home."

"Home?" she asked. "What do you mean, home? You don't live here, you know. You don't owe us anything."

"Well," I stammered. "Next year, when my raise comes through ...."

"What next year?" she asked. And then she added, with a hint of a smile, "What makes you think you are going to be here in a year?"

Not catching the smile, I became flustered.

"Well, uh, well, uh. Uh ...."

I grew silent and we walked to the apartment.

As we entered her house, it was still and quiet. The kids were playing outside, and the place was empty. I put my bags on the kitchen table, turned around, took her bag and put it on the floor. Still facing her, I closed the door behind her and put my hands on either side of her head. I leaned in close and whispered.

"Marry me?"

She returned my closeness by smiling and saying one word.

"When?" (She always did have a talent for understatement.)

"I can get the license on Monday. How about Tuesday?"

"I'll call Lorrie."

"I'll wait," I said. "Then we can tell the kids. Together."

I have had people tell me that that was not a very romantic way to propose, but I disagree. I will never forget the way I felt, the smile in my heart, or in her eyes. No, the proposal was perfect.

From small beginnings....

Mr. and Mrs. Bob and Karen Hendrickson

After the wedding, I learned quickly about kids. They were still young, but two years apart from each other at five years old, seven years old, and nine years old. One of the first things I learned was that three children from the same mother and father could not have been any more different from one another than peanut butter, macaroni, and dog food.

I had to learn different parenting techniques for each of them. They were individuals and would not let me forget it. No two were alike. The most important things they had in common were the need to be loved, have a secure home, and live in a stable family environment. Most of all, I had to try and figure a way to make them comfortable with their new father. If I were able to do that, everything would fall into place. For me, it was largely just trying to understand how to give them what they needed. Whitney, Andrea, and Kyle eventually allowed me to be a part of their lives. I am so grateful they did because it made me a much better person than I was before.

So that crossing turned out to be a great success for me personally. I think it was for the three kids as well. I also learned that becoming a father was no cost to me at all. It was a blessing that keeps on giving back to me 10 times over.

I will never forget how important Karen was in the process. I could never have done it or any part of it without her. For 20 years, I looked at her as the expert in everything "child" because she knew so much more than I. It's only with the benefit of hindsight, now, that I realize she was playing without a net, just like me. I guess she just faked it better than I did.

Becoming a father to the three of them and, eventually, to Lucas, was the best crossing I ever made.

Our new family
Me, Karen, Whitney, Andrea, and Kyle

17

THE AIRLINE OF THE STARS

The Giza Pyramids on approach to Cairo International Airport

As I taxied the MD-80 to the parking gate after landing in Miami International Airport, I marveled at how good it felt. No dream this time. No "giant hands." Just mine, on the controls. And sometime within the next 25 minutes, I would learn my fate.

The date was April 12, 2001, and this was planned to be the last day of my Captain Upgrade Training program at

TWA. This was also the next-to-last flight for us that day. If the check airman in the right seat approved of everything I had done over the past three days (and I do mean everything), he would claim the final leg going back to JFK for his own currency items. I would have passed on my first attempt at upgrading to Captain at TWA. If not, I would face more training, followed by another three-day check ride. Fail that three times in a row, and the upgrade candidate not only lost his chance at being a TWA Captain, he or she would lose their job as a pilot at the airline! TWA was not interested in pilots who could not advance in their careers. TWA claimed they always hired future Captains. They felt a First Officer who could not upgrade to Captain was not good enough to keep flying for TWA.

Some failing candidates were allowed to continue working for the airline as flight engineers and most pilots passed eventually, but about 25 percent did not and found themselves looking for a job. So, the stakes for a pilot, like me, who had accepted the challenge of up-or-out, could not have been any higher.

It had been a good three days. Hank, my check airman, was personable and fun to be with. It was his job to be an excellent co-pilot, but only that. I had to be in charge, give orders and see that they were carried out (all under normal circumstances). The evaluation of my performance under abnormal circumstances had taken place in the MD-80 flight simulator.

A flight simulator is not used by aircrews for training because it is any cheaper than the real thing. In fact, a modern advanced flight simulator costs many times more to operate, per hour, than the actual airplane. The difference is that there are no passengers aboard a simulator. When a pilot learns something the hard way, resulting in a crash in the simulator, the crew walks away, the instructor walks away, and the only thing that needs repair is the pilot's ego. The flight simulator is where the upgrading pilot must survive bad copilots, broken airplanes, un-forecast weather, sick passengers, and whatever Machiavellian scheme the sim operator can think of. Four hours in the sim can be like 8 to 12 hours of hard work because the sim instructors want to put crews under stress to see if they can take it and still perform their functions as flight crew members. This is very important. If pilots can't prove they are able to perform, they are out. It is just that simple. I do not know of any pilot who claims to enjoy going through simulator training, even though they acknowledge its value.

Because of the extraordinarily high consequences for poor performance, the airlines cannot afford to hire anyone but the most competent individuals to pilot their aircraft. There is no attempt to give anyone an easier time because of any reason of sex, ethnicity, religion, etc. If any candidate, regardless of any special background they might have, cannot do the job, they aren't given the job. I like the simplicity of that because we knew that that our fellow crewmembers were more than competent in their jobs. That is a wonderful and absolutely necessary realization.

Knowing, without a doubt, that every person on the crew was a top notch performer was the responsibility of the check airmen that administered their check-rides.. They were the gate-keepers. If a candidate could not convince the check airman that the check airman's family would be safe flying with this individual, then no amount of privilege, political pressure or nepotism would sway the final outcome of the check-ride. While hiring decisions were influenced by many things, there was only one thing that determined the outcome of the final check for any crew member and that was this: "Would I put my family on an airplane with this person?"

This was the same measure I applied to check rides throughout my 43 years in giving and receiving them.

Trans World Airlines Boeing 747

I had been hired in October of 1989, just after I had left the Air Force. Like every other pilot on the TWA property, I started at the bottom ... except that I didn't. During my interviews with the TWA hiring folks, they noted my background of 6,000+ hours of heavy-jet time, mostly over the Atlantic Ocean. So, when they offered me the job, it was as a flight engineer (FE) on the Boeing 747 jumbo jet. That meant I would jump the list of all engineers employed in smaller airplanes at TWA and I would go straight to the 747 FE list. I was still junior to FEs who were hired before me, but a normal FE could not "bump" me off the 747, even with their higher seniority. This saved TWA a lot of training money. The Boeing 747 for its part, was also known as the Queen of the Sky, since it was the largest commercial jet airliner in the world in 1989.

I felt like a minion serving a Jurassic beast whenever I was around the Boeing 747. It was so big and TWA flew the 100 and the 200 versions of the 747.

Go ahead. Ask me what that one does!

For me, being an FE on the 747 was like a two-edged-sword. The airplane was the most fun, it went to all of the best places, and the service provided by the first-class flight attendants was beyond anything I ever knew. The only down-side was that I was the second most junior person on the list of 747 FEs, and that meant that I could not hold a regular schedule. I flew reserve, meaning I might get called out for a flight on as little as two hours' notice. Sometimes I had more time to get there, but that was about it. In six years, I never held a regular schedule on the 747.

Bu that also meant that I got all of the oddball weird things that only a reservist like me could pick up. For instance, I was one of the first FEs at TWA to begin flying the Civil Reserve Air Fleet (CRAF) during Desert Shield and Desert Storm in 1990-1991. I flew every other day, five hours in and five hours out of the war zone, delivering U.S. troops to the fray. We did this for six months and I was logging so much flight time that I had to be taken off the mission occasionally to remain within FAA maximum flight hour guidelines.

I also flew on charters. One Saturday in the spring, we flew a special flight over to Venice, arriving on a Saturday morning. There are usually 16-17 crewmembers on a 747. We had 16-17 people that afternoon on our impromptu wanderings around Venice, Italy on a beautiful springtime afternoon. If I was having difficulty finding a romantic place for my honeymoon, this would be it! I love Venice.

I also love Paris. It was on a flight to Paris that I had an opportunity to do something really special. I was in my crash pad in Valley Stream, New York about six miles from the JFK airport watching the television when the phone rang.

"Flight Engineer Hendrickson, please."

"Speaking."

"I have a good one for you here, Bob," the scheduler said.

"Yeah, well you'd better hurry. It's nine o'clock and all of our flights from JFK are gone. What do you have?"

"It is an equipment substitution. We need a 747 crew in Paris to fly Flight 801 back home tomorrow evening. It was a 767, but now it is going to be a 747 and so, we need a 747 crew there to cover the flight back."

"Tomorrow? How are you going to pull that one off? Like I said, our flights are all gone. Flying even the first flight tomorrow doesn't give us the required rest. We've been through this so many times flying against the time zones. What's different today?"

"You, the Captain, and the First Officer (FO) are going to Paris tomorrow morning ..." he paused for effect "... on the Concorde!"

"Yeah? Cool!"

"Yeah," he said. "You leave here tomorrow at 8 am and you arrive in Paris three hours later. The local time there should be about 5 pm. Flight 801 flies back to JFK at 7 pm.

"How do we get the tickets? That's obviously Air France," I asked him.

"We are making your reservations as we speak. Just walk up to the counter and sign the invoice, and go," he said.

The walk-up fare for my ticket was $7,146.00 in 1995 dollars but the plan worked like a champ. We had proven that it could be done, albeit expensively.

The Concorde was undoubtedly the most advanced flying machine I have ever been on. The windows were small, about 5 inches across. The small cabin suited me, but might have been claustrophobic for some. The 747 I flew had 424 seats and 13 Flight Attendants, a ratio of 32 passengers for every flight attendant. With a capacity of 100 First Class seats and 10 Flight Attendants onboard, the ratio in the Concorde was a much smaller 10 to 1.

Finally, when the aircraft is at cruising altitude above 50,000 feet, the door frames or other metal parts that are in contact with the outside of the airplane are hot. In most airplanes, the outside air temperature at cruising altitude might be -67 degrees centigrade and it is similar for the Concorde, but instead of being cold, the frictional heating caused by the Mach 2.5 supersonic cruise speed of the Concorde makes the skin of the airplane heat up to +99 degrees centigrade. It is the design limit for the airplane, and it determines the cruise speed for the airplane. Faster is hotter, but never exceed 99 degrees C.

After I completed six years as a Flight Engineer on the 747, I was senior enough to upgrade to be a co-pilot, known in the civilian world as a First Officer FO . I upgraded onto the Boeing 727 First Officer's seat. A few years later, I moved over to the newer and smaller MD-80 and then the Boeing 767 and the Boeing 757. These two airplanes shared their type rating. This meant that the cockpits were virtually identical, so holding a rating on one automatically included the other.

One other perk of the First Officer job on the 757 and 767 was that the First Officer, on very long, overwater flights was required to move over (physically) to the Captain's seat during cruise flight so the Captain could rest. The First Officer pretending to be a Captain could not takeoff or land from the left seat. That was reserved for the Captain, only. But, during this part of the flight, he became known as an International Relief Officer, and acted for the Captain. Another First Officer who was along on the flight for that purpose, performed the First Officer's duties until the captain returned to the cockpit. For those of us who got to do this job, it was like being a practice-captain. And, at TWA, it meant that the International /First Officer's (like me) were required to receive a Captain Checkout from the training department. The FAA, officially, considered us captains and gave us a type rating (a captain's license) in the 757 and 767. Thar qualification was a great door-opener later in my aviation career.

When I upgraded to the 767 as a First Officer, I was back on international flights! I loved "international." Going out and managing myself in a foreign country, speaking what I could of the language, and learning about another culture was the end-all for me. I was having so much fun, and the money had finally risen to "fairly bad" instead of just "terrible."

Then one night in Cairo, I had just returned from the marketplace to our hotel at the Nile Hilton. I plugged in my computer and started looking at the pilot's read file. The read file was the source for all official company news, like who just got an upgrade slot. And there I was,

HENDRICKSON, RP, 12591, CA MD8 07 MAR. Simply put, this code meant that Robert Hendrickson, employee number12591, was awarded a captain upgrade slot on the MD-80 aircraft beginning on March 7th. (The year was 2001.)

It took me three months from the class start date to graduation as a TWA Captain. There was a lot more to learn than dealing with balky airplanes. The Captain had to be everybody's everything. The Captain had to be the one in the cockpit who caught all of the mistakes that a new first

Officer fresh out of school and no experience will make. The Captain must know a few things about every destination that he might fly to and all of the major rivers, cities, landmarks, and mountain ranges. As Captain, I needed to know not only what the FAA regulations all said but where I could find the appropriate reference quickly and without fail. The Captain must deal with the crew, passengers, ground crew, gate agents, the airline company, and the Feds. We at TWA were proud of our Captains. When that first Officer Graduated from PUP (Pilot Upgrade Program) as a Captain, he or she was fully qualified. No on-the-job-training required! As the artillery officers in the Army always said, "A Full Up Round." Just load and pull the trigger.

As we taxied into the gate area in Miami, the ground crew smoothly motioned us forward until we were perfectly placed and issued the stop command, which I did.

"Okay, brakes set, there's the external (meaning that the ground crew had plugged in the electrical power from the gate). I looked up as Hank checked the quality of the power.

"Good on the power," he offered.

"I concur." I said.

The lights flashed as we changed over the airplane's power source from the engines to the external power.

"Let's get the seatbelt light," I directed.

"All good," he said.

"Okay. Let's shut 'em down and complete the Parking Checklist down to the line."

All of that was just a fancy way of saying that we were planning to turn the aircraft over to ourselves. It was the right way to get the airplane ready to go again, even after it was just freshly parked at the gate.

With the words "Parking Checklist Complete" the check ride was over. I looked at Hank in anticipation. Either I made it, or I needed to try again. I was all ready for the "speech," but I needed to know which seat I would be riding home in. Would it be left or right?

Hank looked back at me with a sardonic grin on his face and I wondered, *what was up?* For a moment, I thought he was leaning forward to tell me some kind of secret, but instead, he reached back to the back side of the center console and picked up the handset for the Public Address System on the plane. He turned it on and smiled at me.

"Ladies and Gentlemen. Welcome to Miami where the temperature is 78 degrees. We hope you have enjoyed this flight and we thank you for your business." He paused. "As you go by the cockpit door on your way out, please say hello to Captain Bob Hendrickson, TWA's newest Captain. He just passed his final check ride two minutes ago."

Then turning to me with a mock serious expression, he said, "You need to get in the door and say 'hi' to all those people."

Hank is presenting me with a set of TWA Captain's wings engraved with my name.

I had passed many check rides in my life. I had taken many tests. Right up to that moment, I would have told anyone that, by comparison, this wasn't the most important test I had ever passed. I had been a Tanker Task Force Commander in the Air Force, in charge of up to 20 airplanes crossing the Atlantic together. After that level of responsibility, I thought this would be no big deal. I was wrong!

As I stood in the doorway, looking at the faces as they passed me by as they went out of the airplane, my breath caught in my throat. I found it hard to breathe. This little "nothing" of upgrading to Captain that was not supposed to be difficult for me, was. It had taxed me. My lessons, my skills, my abilities, and my talents were all on show and I could not hide from the program. They got all of me and I was unexpectedly moved, more than I ever thought I would be when so many people found me okay with a checkmark. I was now in a very elite group. Captain at TWA. A major, legacy airline in the United States. And the "Airline of the Stars."

Why the Airline of the Stars? Because of Howard Hughes, mostly. He cut a very wide swath in Hollywood, and he owned TWA. It was a natural occurrence that the airline would become the Airline of the Stars. When I was a pilot at TWA, all of the employees were very proud of the fact that it seemed like all of the Hollywood stars wanted to fly TWA and they were very easy to coax into the range of a camera.

It was a lot of fun and very fulfilling, but like so many of the best things in my life, it seemed that this, too, would be short-lived.

18

"YOU WANT TO FEED HIM?"

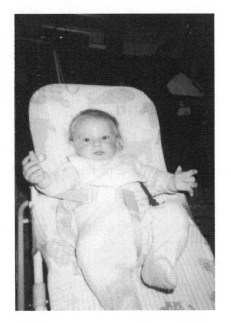

Lucas at two months old

Karen and I were a good team and we worked hard over the next few years to carve out a place for our little family. In February 1999, while she was working at the Out-Patient Oncology Clinic, she came in contact with Peter (not his real name), a patient who had a problem. Not his disease – that was in remission. It was everything else in his life that was a total train wreck.

He was the father of a two-month-old baby boy, but the infant's mother had died two weeks earlier. Peter was unemployed and was soon to be homeless as well.

Karen's co-workers encouraged her to help him out and see if she could get him a job in the small town where she and Peter both lived.

Karen was not familiar with his case, but she offered to baby-sit on the weekends so that he could get a job.

As soon as Karen got home that evening, she talked the situation over with me.

"What do you mean, a two-month-old?" I laughed. "I'm forty-six years old and I've never changed a diaper in my life! I don't know the first thing about babies!"

"It's time you learned," she smiled. "You're probably going to have grandchildren soon. You need to know what to do. Besides," she said, serious now, "this little guy needs help. Maybe we could do some good. It's not like we give a lot to charities."

"Yeah, I know. It's just scary, that's all. Babies scare me."

"You'll do fine," she said.

One Friday afternoon after that, when Karen got home from work, we drove to Peter's apartment. For a few more weeks, Peter still lived in his late girlfriend's apartment in The Gardens apartment complex.

"The Gardens" existed seemingly to prove the so-called 90-10 rule. The 90-10 rule states that 90 percent of a police department's time is spent on 10 percent of the population. Those 10 percent, in our town, lived in The Gardens. Whenever arrests were made for things like drugs, prostitution, theft, or family disturbances, it was a safe bet that the location was somewhere in The Gardens.

The apartment units had a bombed-out appearance, and no grass grew in the spaces between the buildings. Dirty-faced children in ragged clothing played in the streets or in the grimy snow with their broken toys while acid rock or rap music rumbled across the common areas from myriad sources. To be sure, not everyone living in The Gardens was a criminal or an abuser. It just seemed that way.

When we knocked on Peter's door at the appointed time to pick up the baby, there was no answer. A quick peek in the front window, however, revealed a tiny infant in a wind-up swing tick-tocking back and forth in front of the stereo. The music was loud enough to rattle the windows now and then with the heavy bass line. The infant did not seem to notice.

Karen knocked again. Still no answer.

"What do we do now?" I asked.

"I don't know," Karen replied.

Looking in the front window, again, and contemplating our dilemma, we saw the back door to the apartment open and Peter walked in. We tapped on the window. Peter looked up and, seeing us, walked toward the front door. On the way, he turned down the volume on the stereo.

When Peter opened the door, the smell of marijuana and Peter's glassy eyes answered any questions about what he had been doing. Karen and I were just beginning to learn a little bit about Peter's past.

According to others who had known him longer, Peter was a petty criminal. What one of our friends called a ne'er-do-well. His biggest problem was that he was not as smart as he thought. He got caught a lot. And then there was his mean streak. His first trip to the state penitentiary was when he had beaten his mother almost to death. He went to jail for that when he was 15 years old, and he had not really been out of jail for any extended period since then. He was now 29. Karen and I had talked about all of these things as we learned them. These revelations were disturbing but I think we both felt that Lucas needed us.

Karen spoke first.

"Hi, Peter. Sorry to look like a couple of snoops, but we saw Lucas and we just wondered where you were."

'Oh," he said. "I was just next door at Benita's place."

Noticing the baby in the swing, he said "Oh yeah, Lucas. Well, he cries if I just leave him alone, so I turn on the music good and loud and it keeps him quiet. I guess he likes it."

"Did you still want us to take Lucas for the weekend?" Karen asked.

"Yeah, sure!" Peter was eager. "Let me get his stuff."

I carried Lucas' car seat out to the car and strapped it into the back seat while Karen collected Lucas and his diaper bag.

"Okay, Peter. We'll have him back Sunday evening."

"Yeah, okay," he replied.

As the three of us, (Karen, Lucas, and I drove away), I was silent.

"Well?" asked Karen.

"Well, what?" I answered.

"Well, out with it. You have something to say? Usually, when you're silent it means you've got something to say."

"I don't know. I guess I'm just stunned, that's all. I never had any idea .... "

"Let's just get this little boy home and clean him up and feed him," she said.

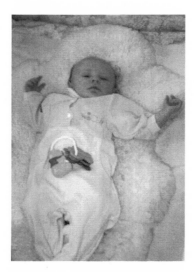

Lucas as an infant during his first visit to our home

When we got home, Karen picked up Lucas and headed inside, leaving me to gather up the diaper bag.

Our fourteen-year-old son, Kyle was waiting at the door when we arrived.

"What's for dinner?" he asked. Then, looking at Lucas, he added "So, this is the kid?"

"Yeah," I said. Turning to Karen, I asked "How about I make dinner, while you go take care of Lucas?"

"How about you just order pizza and come up and help me?" she replied.

"Oh, yeah, that's a good idea," I replied. So, I ordered the standard Hendrickson family fare of two large pizzas and headed upstairs after Karen.

I honestly had never seen a two-month-old infant up close before, so I really had no measure of what one should look like. As I looked at Lucas, the first thing I saw was a wet, goopy diaper. Karen had removed it and was gently wiping away the mess from his skin. Lucas didn't like the procedure and was crying and squirming around in pain and discomfort. His cries, however, were not very loud and his squirms were ineffectual. I noticed that the skin all over his body was splotchy and there was angry redness all over his bottom, his groin, and his neck. He was also bleeding from the area beneath his chin.

"Why is he bleeding there?" I asked.

"Because he hasn't been cleaned in that spot and his skin is all broken down," she replied. "And besides, he lives and sleeps in that damned car seat. He's never raised his head up, and the skin under his chin is just a mess."

Karen continued to clean up the little boy and I helped when I could. When we finished, we put some over-the-counter ointments and creams on his skin. When Karen was satisfied, we carried him downstairs where Kyle and his 16 year-old sister, Andrea were just finishing off the two large pizzas.

"Oh, he's soooo cute!" bubbled Andrea. "He's pretty small, though."

Karen looked at me. "Ever mixed formula?" she asked.

"Nope, but I can read directions if it's not too tricky."

"It's not," she said. "Just make sure it's body temperature."

"Okay," I said. "I've seen that on TV. I can do that."

I went to the kitchen to mix the formula while Karen introduced Lucas to Andrea and Kyle. When I re-emerged with the formula in hand, Karen tested it on her arm and found it to be just right. Then she asked me, "You want to feed him?"

Karen with Lucas at 2 months old

"No way!" I replied. "You'd better demonstrate first."

Karen took the baby expertly into the crook of her left arm and with her right hand, held the bottle to Lucas' mouth.

"Wow, he was hungry!" she said as Lucas devoured the formula. Shortly, however, Lucas stopped eating and, in a few moments, all of the formula came right back up again running down his chin and onto the neck of his tee shirt. As Karen cleaned him up, she said: "Okay, that explains a lot. I'll bet he just can't tolerate that kind of formula."

"There are different kinds?" I asked.

"Of course." she said. "If he can't tolerate this and he throws it up all the time, it would explain why his neck is all broken down and he's underweight. Go to the store and buy this kind." She wrote the name on a piece of paper.

"Okay. Be right back."

I immediately went to the store and bought the formula that Karen had specified. Her intuition proved to be exactly right. When I returned with the correct formula, I went into the kitchen and mixed it up.

"Here," I said. "Try this."

Lucas did great with the new formula. Soon after he had the new bottle, he was sleeping peacefully in Karen's arm.

As Karen watched him sleep, I was watching Karen. "Don't fall in love with that little baby," I said. "You are going to wind up with him."

"No. Three is plenty," she said.

But, fall in love with him she did, and so did I.

Soon, Peter was back in jail and we needed a legal way to keep Lucas with us until what, we did not know. So, we became Legal Guardians to Lucas. As Legal Guardians, we were ordered by the court to take care of Lucas "as if he was our own." We were to provide a home for Lucas, love him, keep him from harm, and submit annual reports to the court to prove that we were doing all of those things.

Over the next five years, we tried several times to find a situation for Peter and Lucas to reunite. We tried to set up visitations for them at a visitation center in town, but Peter did not want to pay the $10 per visit. We carried Lucas out to the county jail to visit with Peter periodically, but Lucas crawled under a chair and hid from Peter.

There was simply no way that Peter was ever going to get Lucas back if Peter never got out of jail so, for those five years, we fought to keep Lucas safe and to make sure he was loved. The judge had tried a number of times over that period to take Lucas and return him to Peter on no better grounds than "blood is thicker than water," although what that meant was unclear to us. Fortunately, for us and for Lucas, every time he tried, Peter was back in jail for a new reason.

These legal struggles to give Lucas a stable home were insanely expensive. There were studies to determine our suitability as parents. There were psychological evaluations on Lucas, our other children, and of course, on Karen and me. Finally, there were the monthly visits to the jail, which were miserable for all of us. Soon, we were nearing the end of all our money, if not our willingness to fight. Almost six years had come and gone, and all of our savings went by in the blink of an eye.

When American Airlines reacted to 9/11, they closed all of the East Coast domiciles for their pilots who had flown for TWA. That meant that we were now compelled to move to St Louis, Missouri if I was to continue to fly for TWA/American. It was time. It was time for Karen and me to end the temporary situation that we were in with Lucas. It was time to make our declaration. It was time to adopt Lucas. We knew that we faced opposition from Peter, the judge, history, prejudice, and precedent. If ever there were a Crossing filled with danger, mystery, unknown outcomes and unknowable costs for all of us, this was it.

With faith in each other, and a plan that we hoped would succeed, Karen and I committed ourselves to the fight, took one another's hands and made the leap into the abyss.

When we asked our lawyer what we were going to do, she showed us the pertinent statutes which said,

"The guardian shall establish the domicile of the minor child, within or without the State of New Hampshire. The guardian(s) will contact a court of competent jurisdiction at the new domicile which will contact the court of relieving jurisdiction and assume responsibility for the guardianship in the new domicile." In other words, go now, tell later.

So we moved to St. Louis and contacted the Family Court there.

We immediately were contacted by the court back home to appear there, within 14 days. When we arrived, the courtroom was the same as it always was: dark, foreboding, and full of angst and danger.

After the preliminaries, the judge got right to the point.

"Where's the boy?" he asked.

"Your honor," our lawyer said, "Lucas is back home in St. Louis. Your letter only specified the Hendricksons, so he has remained at home this time. As you know, your honor, the Hendricksons' travel is not free. It costs much less not to bring Lucas if it is not necessary."

The judge grumbled and looked at her proffered sheet of paper. "I know he flies for free. He's an airline pilot. (Meaning me)"

"Your Honor, this trip back from St. Louis costs them a great deal in auto rentals, hotels, meals, and so forth. It comes to about $1,000 per trip."

The judge seemed incredulous. "So, about all I have remaining is what, Contempt of Court?"

Abruptly, the judge spoke to us, fuming, "Mr. and Mrs. Hendrickson, what you did here was illegal, unwise, borderline stupid, and it displeases the court. If I ever see you back in front of this bench for these kinds of shenanigans, I will take that little boy and you two will rot in jail until I feel like letting you out!"

Totally defeated, he added to the lawyers present, "I think you all should work something out. Settle this. Soon!"

We all flinched as the gavel came down with a loud bang. "Dismissed!"

A few days later, I called the Guardian AD Litem. This is Lucas' lawyer who, in theory, is supposed to represent Lucas.

I wondered aloud at him, "Why do you think this little boy would be better off with Peter? Lucas knows us, and us alone, as his Mom and Dad. Peter is a prisoner at the county jail. Where is he supposed to keep Lucas?"

The Guardian Ad Litem was playing very cool.

"Well, I think the judge feels blood is thicker than water."

"Yeah, well, what can I do to break our impasse?

"You could give me $1,000. I think that would do it. Then I will recommend to the judge that I think the boy should go with you."

"Really? A thousand dollars?"

I could only think of the tens of thousands Karen and I had already spent

"Sure," I said. "You put that in writing, and I will do it!"

"You got it," he said.

This lawyer sent me a handwritten note on his office stationery, which said that he would recommend favorably to the judge in return for $1,000 from me. "Extortion" is the word that came to my mind but I suppose I was just being naive.

I sent the note to the judge and asked him what he thought of that!

"I think you should pay the man," he replied.

I was flabbergasted, but I wrote the check.

That was the easiest check for $1,000 I ever wrote.

Karen and I were soon going back to St. Louis to live with Lucas, and importantly, a new court. Six months later, we were back in court. But now, it was St. Louis Family Court. We had filed for adoption based on Peter's abandonment. It had been six months without a card, a call, or any attempt on his part to make any kind of contact at all with Lucas.

This room was nothing like the dark, threatening court in our old home town. This place was more like a conference room. It had a few, very functional tables arranged in a large horseshoe shape and a desk in the corner where a clerk sat doing some kind of mysterious paperwork. The judge was sitting at one of the functional tables just like the one where I sat. The chairs were filled with lawyers and there was not a single spectator in the room. The walls were white and there wasn't a column anywhere in sight.

This was day two of the proceedings.

We were directly across from the judge, where we had been sitting for two days. Peter was on the phone from the county jail. Karen sat to my left and Lucas sat between us. The lawyers had just finished making their closing arguments and all eyes were on the Family Court judge.

The judge shuffled a few papers in front of her and made a notation of some kind on one of them.

"Thank you Peter. Your lawyer will contact you with my verdict. Good bye." She hung up the phone.

I looked over at Karen and our eyes met.

Karen's face was ashen, and she looked slightly ill. It had been an incredibly difficult six years and Karen was terrified. I could only imagine how I looked.

The judge made another notation on her folder and then cleared her throat. She looked up and spoke to the young boy sitting in front of her.

"Well, what do YOU want, Lucas?"

Lucas turned to me with a questioning look on his face. "Go ahead," I said.

Lucas looked back at the judge and said quietly, "I want to be 'doptid.'"

For the first time in two days, the judge smiled.

"Well, Lucas. You've got your wish. Because of all of the things that we have talked about here in this room for the last two days, I believe that granting this adoption for you is the best thing I can do. So that is what I am going to do right now."

She paused.

"Lucas, from now on, your name will be Lucas Robert Hendrickson. Your parents here will continue to be your Mom and Dad, just as if you had been born their son. You can go back home with them, to your home, and continue being their son. But now, it's forever. Do you understand?"

149

"Uh huh," Lucas said.

"Okay," said the magistrate to the new parents. "Take care of this little boy. This court is adjourned."

"All rise," said the clerk, and the tension that had surrounded the courtroom for two days, lifted as a fog before the morning sun. For the first time in so many years, I began to realize that the young boy beside me was finally catching a break. The courtroom began to slowly dissolve in the tears that I had promised myself would not come.

As the lawyers began shuffling their papers and restoring them to their bulging folders, the hand shaking began and serious voices became ebullient and self-congratulatory. Lucas looked at me and whispered.

"Daddy, can we go now? I'm hungry."

Lucas wanted a Happy Meal.

Such is the power of a six-year-old, that the most dramatic events of a tumultuous life were reduced to minor annoyances in the face of yet another cheeseburger and a Teenage Mutant Ninja Turtle toy from McDonald's. I looked at Lucas and, once again, wondered at the power of a single life. I wondered at how such a small person had the power to change the life course of so many around him and yet be no more concerned about it than his next "Raphael" or "Donatello" toy.

Lucas had indeed changed the course of our lives in ways that were dramatic, heartbreaking, funny, sometimes devastating, and always, seemingly, out of our control. Sometimes, we likened our experience to an emotional roller coaster, but it was more like five years of Russian roulette with the life of a helpless child at the end of the barrel.

Lucas had survived, however. He had survived because of a bit of luck, but mostly the tenacity of two people who knew nothing about the law or children's issues going in, but who had learned quickly. Two normal people who were only trying to do what they naively thought was "the right thing to do."

And so it was, that one child was saved, and a family of 5 became a family of 6.

"Sure, Spud. Let's go," I said.

Karen, Lucas Robert Hendrickson and I left the court-room, turning a corner in the hallway and in our lives and walked out the door into the crisp, February air. Our small family was going to McDonald's in search of another Happy Meal and Lucas was bouncing.

Lucas

Karen and I had to watch over our shoulders from that day forward. Peter had let it be known to us and to a number of intervening police that he wanted to make Karen and me pay for "stealing" his child. He would sit outside our home, wherever we lived, and call us on the telephone to gloat that he was out front, watching us, and he had a gun. For the next ten years, I carried a concealed .40 caliber Glock, and Karen carried a 9 mm Glock. We lived Lucas's childhood in fear.

19

END GAME

It was a crisp breezy day in early September of 2009. The sun's arc was getting lower in the sky and the air in the shade was cool and damp. The grass and trees were still green, but their headlong summer growth had slowed in the signs of fall were all around.

I was outside, stacking the firewood. Three weeks before, a local man had backed his large truck into our driveway and unceremoniously deposited four large cords of cut and split firewood in a pile in the yard. I knew I needed to get the wood into the lean-to shed against the garage and stack it so it would have a chance to dry out before the winter made that impossible.

Our house was heated primarily by a wood stove in the living room. It was important that there was an ample supply of dry firewood available so that we did not find it necessary to turn on the electric heaters in the house. Electric rates in Maine were so high that we simply could not afford it.

I stopped to watch a formation of geese headed south overhead. I pulled off my work gloves and sat down on one of the large rocks dotted around the property. As I sipped from my glass of water, I reflected on the past year.

Lucas' adoption had finally become official on March 1, 2004 and so, we celebrated the occasion. It was now more than five years since a tiny, bruised, smelly baby had first come into our lives. A few of our friends who had supported us throughout this long ordeal attended. I will never forget how my close friends Rick and Martha Packard flew up from Washington, DC just for this celebration. They had been, and still remain, amazing friends.

The summer had passed in a blur of sunny afternoons and ice cream cones; then suddenly on September 1, Lucas boarded a big yellow school bus and attended his very first day of kindergarten. I smiled thinking of how excited Lucas had been sitting in that huge green school bus seat and how it towered over him, making him look ridiculously small and vulnerable.

Just yesterday, Lucas had attended his first soccer practice at the town athletic field. He ran hard and kicked the ball with vigor. I chuckled to myself. I guess little details like which direction to go and what those strange goal-things were for would come later.

I looked at the house and once again saw the signs that it needed to be painted before the long, harsh Maine winter. There were still some windows that needed maintenance and the bushes need to be trimmed. It seemed that there was no end to all the little things that need to be done just to keep everything going.

As I sat contemplating the side of the house, I heard a scrape behind me and a voice.

"Hey, Bob."

My blood ran cold. I knew that voice. I didn't know what to do.

I turned and looked into the face of Peter.

Peter stood beside the woodshed about 15 feet away. How he had gotten so close without being heard, I didn't know. He leaned casually against the shed holding a large black gun in his right hand.

"Uh, hi, Peter," I answered.

This didn't look good. He would not be so bold as to show up here with a gun in his hand unless he had some kind of plan. My mind raced. Well, I thought. Best not to piss him off.

"You know, Lucas isn't here."

153

"I know that," Peter snapped. "You think I'm stupid?"

"No, no, of course not!" I replied.

Well, that didn't work. Now what?

"Uh, what's up?"

I knew it was a useless question, but I was stalling for time. I was looking desperately around for anything I could use as a weapon. Over in the shed, to Peter's left, was a large axe I used to split the firewood. It was about 10 feet away and I knew I didn't have much time.

"You know you been a real pain in my ass for a long time," Peter said. "You stole my son after I trusted you with him. You aren't his family. He belongs to me. It's gonna be really good to finally be rid of you."

"Peter," I said, trying to be as calm as I could. "You know you can't get Lucas back by doing anything to me."

I took a step, as casually as I could, toward the shed

Peter gave a short laugh.

"Shows you what you know, asshole. With you and Karen gone, I'm his only living relative. He may go to foster care for a while, but I'll get him back soon enough."

His voice had become low and sinister.

"Remember what Judge Harvey said: 'Blood is thicker than water.'"

He chuckled at his little joke. He did not know it yet, but his time was running out.

I took another step towards the shed. I was halfway there.

"Not if you're in jail for doing this!"

"Shit!" He laughed again. "I'm on Work Release! I'm officially still in jail! Ha, what a perfect alibi. I'm actually at work at my friend's recycle business right now. He thinks I went over to my girlfriend's house. He will tell the cops I was at work all day, or it's his ass too. No, I've got a perfect alibi, besides ..." his voice got sinister again "... how do you think I killed the little brat's mother? Cops are so stupid."

I took another step toward the shed. I was really close and Peter had distracted himself with his self-congratulations. I only needed something to distract him for just a second so I could grab the axe. Fate seemed to smile at me because, just at that moment, we both heard the crunch of tires on stone. A car was coming up the driveway. Karen and Lucas were home from the store. Peter glanced over to see who it was, and I knew that I wouldn't get another chance. I dove for the axe and grabbed it!

The explosion was loud. I had never heard anything so loud. My ears rang and I smelled smoke. For the moment, I just stood there staring at Peter, trying to understand what had just happened. Peter looked back at me, seemingly, as shocked as I was.

It was confusing. There was no pain, just surprise and confusion.

What the heck was that noise and why had everything just stopped? Why can't I hear anything?

Then I noticed that I couldn't feel my legs anymore. I looked down but could not quite understand why my legs and feet were there, but I could not control them. Then my knees started to bend, and I could not stop them either. Slowly I sank to the ground in the shed. I tried to put my hands out to arrest my fall, but they would not respond either. One hand was still on the shovel handle, the other hanging loosely at my side. I flopped over sideways and came to rest with my head staring at the bottom row of the woodpile. A piece of wood hit me in the side of the face and it hurt.

I could not move, and I could not breathe. Somehow, I knew that the darkness closing around me was death's harbinger. Even though I felt confusion and shock, I knew with absolute clarity I was going to die, here, in this damned shed.

So this was what it was like to die. How absurd. It's not supposed to happen this way!

A wash of emotions began to fill my consciousness. I was sad because I had not finished so much I had planned. Without me here, there was no finishing any of my projects.

What would happen to those? I was embarrassed because this was a really stupid way to die. I could hear them all now. How many people are going to say, "Yeah, well, he brought it upon himself. I told him that guy was dangerous."

Worst of all, I felt guilty. I had failed to protect Karen and Lucas. Peter was going to win, and there was nothing I could do about it now. I had tried my best, and I had failed. I just wanted to cry, I felt so empty inside. I had let everybody down.

As I lay there on my side staring at the woodpile, I was still confused. I could not understand why the numerals "333" were written on the bottom of one particular log. What did they mean and why were they so important? As I stared at the digits trying to understand their significance, the last digit changed to a "4."

3:34

"Are you okay?" It was Karen, speaking to me quietly, in her pillow voice.

"What?" I asked.

"You were having that dream again, weren't you?"

"No," I said. "I'm okay. Go back to sleep."

"Where are you going?" she asked as I got up from the bed.

"I'm going to get something to drink and look in on Luke."

"Love you," she murmured.

"Love you too," I said as I bent over and kissed her on the forehead.

The moon was high in the night sky, and the house was bathed in a dim white light as I quietly padded into Lucas's room. The little boy was sound asleep on his right side, clutching a Care Bear toy to his chest. I pulled the sheet back up over his little body and stroked his hair.

Lucas slept soundly.

20

THE INVESTIGATOR

Here I am examining the left engine
of a Boeing 777 in San Francisco

Ever since the hot day in Arizona where I first picked up a part of a crashed T-38, I knew that it would be an important part of my life to investigate airplane accidents. It was important to the public, my colleagues, and to me that these deaths should not have been in vain. There were lessons to be learned here and I felt that I could really make a difference with my unique background and abilities.

For the past 30 years, I had been learning these lessons and filing them away in my mind. It had taken me until 2001 to finally get selected to fly as a Captain for TWA. Unlike the Air Force, it was a process that had nothing to do with merit and everything to do with seniority. When your number came up on the seniority list, you got one shot at Captain Upgrade. I had made it, finally, and I was thrilled to be there. But it took a cataclysm and some extraordinary circumstances to put me in a position to bring all those experiences together.

When I watched the airplanes fly into the towers on 9/11, I knew immediately that the airline industry was going to be hit hard and I would most likely lose my job as an airline pilot once again. Under the circumstances, it looked more permanent this time. For me as an airline pilot, the timing could not have been worse. When I was furloughed, I was 49 years old and the official furlough date was July 1, 2003.

American Airlines had acquired TWA and all its assets in a wild and crazy buy-out/merger deal that had a huge effect on me. I was placed at the bottom of the American Airlines Pilot Seniority List. That meant instead of being a high seniority pilot with TWA, I now occupied the bottom rung of the American Airlines seniority ladder. After more than 12 years with TWA, I would be one of the first to be furloughed and last to be offered a position when my airline employer rehired!

At the time, the federally mandated retirement age for airline pilots was 60 years old. This meant that even if I went back to the pilot job after my furlough, I would be at the bottom of the huge American Airlines Seniority List and I would have very little time to recoup a Captain's seat, if I ever did at all. Even if I did get back to being a Captain, I would have precious little time, after that, to prepare financially for a mandatory retirement at 60. My window of opportunity for financial security and professional advancement was rapidly closing.

I needed to find another job to support my family. I had not managed to scrape anything together for our retirement, having spent everything on lawyers and the process of adopting Lucas. My savings account was at zero, I had just lost my job, and I now had 11 years left in my airline career and that was it! Financially, we were at rock-bottom, and by all rights I should have been depressed. Yet, I do not think I have ever been happier. I knew exactly what I needed to do and how I would do it.

The furlough notice came into my company-electronic mailbox during a trip to San Diego. We were in and out of there on what is called a "turnaround." We had flown in from St. Louis and after about an hour, we would return to St. Louis.

During a previous airline furlough, I had attended a course in Houston, Texas called the "Displaced Workers Program." This was where I learned how to find a job. I know that sounds incredible that I was new to the process at age 49, but it is not. Like so many people from my generation, finding a job was simply a matter of going to work and staying with the same company forever, advancing (or not), collecting your gold watch after 50 years, and retiring. That paradigm changed and the new reality landed very hard on us baby boomers.

Finding a job is an entire skillset that we, as a society, do not teach our children. How to make a cold call, how to write a resume, how to interview well, and so many other skills have to be taught and learned to become a successful job hunter. These skills have become even more important as jobs have become less permanent. At 49 years old, I needed to put my lessons to work, and land a job.

My first call was to the National Transportation Safety Board (NTSB). I had already done some cursory research and learned who, within that agency, held the hiring decision for the job I wanted. Very quickly, I had the head of Major Investigations on the phone. I told him who I was and my qualifications, and I asked if there might be any openings for a person like me.

"Well, with all of your airline background and heavy airplane experience, you are over-qualified for anything except the Investigator In Charge (IIC) position. The problem is, Bob, those positions are all full right now. We just have six IICs on staff and those openings only occur about once every four or five years, so we do not expect anything to happen soon. Why don't you call the FAA? They investigate accidents, too."

I thanked him for the lead and called the Federal Aviation Administration (FAA).

The FAA is a huge government agency. It employs more than 47,000 people. In order to bring some kind of control to their hiring process, the FAA requires all job applicants to complete a long questionnaire about their job experience, demographics, and abilities. If an applicant passes this computer-scored process, his or her name is placed on "the list." There is no rank ordering to the list. Your name appears there, or it does not. No one in the FAA may hire any person unless their name appears on the list. It became very clear within the first few phone calls that the "list" was sacrosanct. No one would even talk to me on the phone unless and until my name appeared there.

My official date of furlough from American Airlines was July 1, 2003. I spent my last few free days finalizing my resume and getting on the requisite list. On July 2, 2003 at 8:00 a.m. sharp, I shut the door to my home office and began making cold calls.

"Hello? Boston Flight Standards District Office. How may I direct your call?"

"Hi, may I speak to your office manager, please?"

"Certainly. Whom may I say is calling?"

"My name is Bob Hendrickson. Thanks."

Click, Buzz, Ring-Ring.

"Hello? May I help you?

This is where I had about 30 seconds to: 1. Introduce myself; 2. Make a positive impression; and 3. Ask for an interview.

"Hello Mr. (Jones)? My name is Bob Hendrickson. I am looking for a position as an Air Safety Inspector (ASI) with the FAA because, as you probably already know, American Airlines is furloughing their pilots, and I am one of them."

Then, I gave a very brief listing of my experience in the Air Force, my 12 years at TWA, and my dabbling in accident investigation. I wrapped things up by asking for the interview.

"I would like to come and meet with you and your staff so you can have an opportunity to look over my qualifications and see if I might fit into your organization." The whole thing took 30 seconds. Any longer, and I would be wasting the time of the very person I was trying to impress.

By far, the most common reply was, "Are you on the list?"

"Yes, sir."

Then came the second most common statement.

"Well, we aren't hiring right now, anyway."

"Yes, sir, but when you do hire someone, I want to be the person that you turn to first. I hope that you do after we have met and you know what I have to offer. May I stop by sometime at your convenience and give you my resume?"

I found very few office managers who were not willing to meet me on those terms. I had been told that in the bottom-right drawer of their government-issue desk was a stack of resumes representing people just like me who were looking for a job. The sad fact is that most applicants seek the FAA job for 3-5 years before the phone call comes, if it ever does at all.

For he next week, I made cold calls to Flight Standards District Offices (FSDOs) all around the United States. Traveling to in-person interviews was no problem for me as I still had my flight privileges with American Airlines, even though I was furloughed. I started my FAA job search locally, in St. Louis, but quickly branched out to Flight Standards District Offices all over the U.S. I knew my chances of getting a job with the FAA were directly proportional to my willingness to relocate. I had been told that the most important thing was to get the job. Then, later, I could move to a better place if I wanted to. By the end of the first week, I had set up interviews from Dallas to Portland, Maine; and from Boston to LA. I began traveling and spreading resumes into bottom-right drawers all over the country.

Nearing the end of that first month of my search, July 2003, some FAA analyst in Washington, DC looked at his projections for the remainder of the fiscal year and decided that the FAA needed to hire some inspectors. He went to his supervisor with the budget projections and made his case. The supervisor agreed and the word went out to the FSDOs around the country: "Hire now."

Timing is everything. For me, it was amazing. Within three weeks of my furlough from American Airlines, I received firm offers from Boston, Dallas, and Portland, Maine – all on the same day.

I accepted the offer from Portland. It was a smaller FSDO and therefore, I reasoned, more opportunity to stand out than in a larger office. Also, importantly, I wanted to put my sailboat on Casco Bay. Finally, and most important of all, Karen would be near her family in Maine. She had followed my nomadic career around for years. It was now her turn to choose a place where she could be happy. Within days, I had a new job, back with the government, in Maine. Although I took a substantial cut in my pay for the first few years, it was a steady job, and, much to my surprise, the pay got a lot better quickly. Of course, money was not my goal here.

The initial training for practically all Air Safety Inspectors is held in Oklahoma City, Oklahoma, at the FAA Academy. When I returned from my first accident-investigation school, I told everyone in the FSDO that I would take their "accident standby duty" because I wanted to get experience in and build a resume for accident investigation. Many of them took me up on that. As a result, I worked a lot of accidents in my FSDO, and because I volunteered for the extra duty, everyone in the FSDO saw it as a win-win.

Early in 2005, I had been working at the Portland, Maine FSDO for less than two years when the first opening was advertised for an accident investigator in FAA Headquarters in Washington, DC. This was the notice I had been waiting for. The advertised FAA HQ position was with the Accident Investigation Division (AAI-100). AAI-100 was the most elite team of accident investigators in the FAA and, perhaps, in the world. The AAI-100 office consisted of five to seven positions as Investigator In Charge (IIC), one Team Lead, one Director and two administrative positions. The average number of people who worked for AAI-100 was 10-12, max. AAI-100 was small, elite, and generally regarded as being the type of experts who were at the top of author Tom Wolfe's pyramid (as described in his book, *The Right Stuff*).

AAI-100 IICs were also very powerful. Whenever an accident investigation required expertise in a subject area where an AAI-100 investigator felt needed a more expert look, the IIC had the authority to reach out to any of the 47,000 people in the FAA and simply say, "I need you." And that was all it took. These investigators had the power of asking for help from any office in the FAA at any time. In a fatal aircraft accident, nobody refused.

When an investigation was complete, the FAA IIC[4] was required to brief his leadership on the accident, its causes and his proposed corrective action. Very often, that corrective action would consist of sitting down with the proper people in the companies involved and telling them what they needed to fix before they could fly again. Unlike the National Transportation Safety Board (NTSB), who "deter-

---

[4] This gets confusing because the NTSB and the FAA both call their lead person in their investigations the IIC. So, when there is any ambiguity, I will use the terms FAA IIC and NTSB IIC.

mined the probable cause and made recommendations," the FAA – specifically the IIC from AAI-100 – could tell CEOs of billion-dollar corporations, aviation industry experts, and even colleagues within the FAA what they needed to do before flying operations could continue. The AAI-100 Investigator was the "honest broker." He or she could also be a hammer. The NTSB recommended corrective actions. The FAA had the authority to require them.

Because of the agency's critical role, it is required by law that the FAA be afforded the opportunity to go with the NTSB on all aviation-related accidents they investigate. The IIC from AAI-100 does not stand in front of any microphones or TV cameras. Such behavior is specifically discouraged by FAA leadership. Sometimes, corrective action is simpler if the media are NOT involved. The function of AAI-100 is to compel action, not just to recommend it. As a result, FAA IICs worked in relative anonymity, even though they have a powerful regulatory role.

As soon as I heard there was an opening in AAI-100, I applied. The response from Human Resources (HR) was swift and brutal. They told me I could not be hired because they felt I was unqualified for this position. They determined I had not been in the FAA long enough and my current pay grade was too low to make the jump even to the lowest AAI-100 pay grade. The IIC job was just too far of a reach for me to make from my current position. It was at that point I knew I needed to do something, or maybe two somethings ....

Strike one.

The first thing that I needed to address was my pay scale. It was too low. And the second thing I needed to do was to move from Portland, Maine to Washington, DC, to be closer to the job I wanted. Fortunately, I had been sought out by the Washington, DC FSDO for a position there. A group of investors in Washington wanted to certify a new, start-up airline called MAXJet. They wished to operate Boeing 767 airplanes back and forth to Europe as their routes.

In April, 2005, the Washington FSDO needed a fully rated 767 Captain to evaluate them for their suitability. I was not the only 767 Captain the FAA had at the time, but I was available. This was where my FAA Captain's type rating on the Boeing 757/767 helped me get a leg up to s new job. It was a perfect match. By July 2005, I had transferred to "America's FSDO" (as they called themselves) as the Principal Operations Inspector (POI) for MAXJet Airlines. The FSDO was located at the Washington Dulles Airport so the drive to work from Winchester, VA was not too bad, and the pay was one step closer to the AAI-100 position. I was busy and having fun in my new assignment, but I also was on the hunt for the AAI-100 job at FAA Headquarters in downtown DC.

A MAXJet Boeing 767

While working at the FSDO, I made friends with the AAI-100 IICs in Washington, DC. They had so many stories about how many places they had been, and what they had done there; they easily lived up to their reputations. I dropped in about once or twice a month to do lunch or hang out in their bullpen and talk about anything and everything.

We just shot the bull and hung around the water cooler. They knew me and I knew them. My ticket in was my heavy-jet experience. Of all the job applicants the FAA receives, they very rarely get someone who has been a Captain for a large airline. This is easy to understand, because qualified airline Captains would, typically, rather work in the cockpit than behind a government desk.

I hoped I was the perfect person for them. I wanted, desperately, to work here with these people – whom I found fascinating – in a job that was as challenging as it was difficult. I made no secret of my motivation to work in this office. I often walked around the general area of AAI-100 and talked with people who worked close to my hoped-for destination. During one of these walks, I was indeed fortunate to meet a very important person, even though she didn't have an official title that matched her influence. Her name was Roberta Toth.

Roberta was the heart of AAI-100. She was referred to as a clerk, or a secretary, or some other title that underplayed her importance. Yet, she hosted the web page that was visited by every flying safety office in the world every morning. It was easily the most visited page in the FAA, perhaps even the entire U.S. Government. Her page provided information on all accidents, incidents, and occurrences the FAA was involved in. It kept running totals on all important crash and airworthiness data and served as the "one-stop shop" for all accident information the U.S. government knew about.

I found her job to be surprisingly challenging. Imagine this: just determining standardized aircraft nomenclature could be a big problem. An example of this challenge is the Boeing 737. What do you call a 737 when you are putting information into a database that was developed in 1960? Is it an a) B-737, b) b-737, c) b737, d) Boeing 737, e) b-731 (for the -100 model), f) b731, g) B-731, h) b-737-1, i) B-737-100, or j) something else? I saw all of these methods for identifying THE SAME EXACT AIRPLANE! How could a researcher possibly find anything out of that data base if they didn't know what to call the airplane involved? The answer is a common taxonomy. That is, settle on one way you might want to call a 737 today, and stick to it. Otherwise, researchers will confront a database that resembles a Tower of Babel, from which nothing useful can be found.

Having such a huge database and being careful to control every little bit of data that goes into it requires strict quality control. I enjoyed learning about her system and, although I did not know it, Roberta was one of the main reasons that, after quite a few attempts, I finally got the job in AAI-100.

Another year passed and suddenly, there was another opening at AAI-100, and I applied for it, as I had done previously. As before, my application was not sent along with the "qualified" applicants as chosen by Human Resources (HR). This time, though, there was a difference. The team lead for AAI-100 was a man named Bob Drake. He looked at the list of qualified applicants and when he did not see my name listed, he marched directly down to the HR office and asked "How come this name is not on the list? He is certainly qualified, and we want to interview him."

The HR person cited my lack of time in the FAA – I only had three years versus some others who had been with the agency much longer. Plus, there were literally hundreds of applicants for the position. HR felt they had cut it down to 65 of the most qualified applicants, *in their opinion.* Bob Drake stood his ground, however, and demanded to know why I was not on the list.

In the end, HR could not come up with a good reason. Whatever the reason was, I would not have even been considered if it had not been for the fact that Bob Drake went to bat for "that guy, Bob" who came around every couple of weeks and just sat and ate lunch or traded war stories with the IICs. When he mentioned what happened in conference later that day, Roberta almost came out of her chair.

"Bob Hendrickson?" she asked. "I know him! He's so smart! You have GOT to hire him." From that point on, if my name was in discussion, Roberta was singing my praises. I think she did more to get me into AAI-100 than any other single person.

I made the short list of 65 from hundreds of applicants. Now I had to be selected for an interview with the panel. From the list of 65, they chose 10 for the panel interview. The panel consisted of one AAI-100 person, acting as a moderator, and four senior people, none of whom worked in AAI-100. The goal was to see if the applicants could communicate with people from different backgrounds and different areas of expertise without injecting their own expectations, acronyms, arcane language, and unfounded opinions into the mix. They were looking for a person who could work with anyone and produce results.

One week later, I was asked to come downtown to meet with the Director of AAI. There were five of us who had made that cut.

Two weeks later, in my mail, I received the letter:

"Dear Bob, I want to personally thank you for your participation in our interview process. Although you were very qualified, we had so many highly qualified...." You can imagine the rest.

I wondered what I needed to change for the next time.

Swing and a miss. Strike two!

Two days later, I received the most extraordinary call from the Director of AAI.

"Bob, Hi. This is Hooper Harris. How are you?"

"Hi, Hooper. What's up?"

"Well, Bob. You know the process. We sent our selection down to HR and they sent out the letters last week. Did you get yours?"

"Yeah, I did. Well, next time."

I chuckled, trying to cover up my disappointment, adding, "You know, I am just going to keep applying, right?"

"Well, you might not need to," he said. "They made a mistake."

"What?"

"They offered the job to someone else on the list. Someone we did not select. We selected you."

"Wow! So, what now?" I asked. "Can they do that?"

"Technically, yes. But I've never seen it.

"The other applicant was (he named her). I already called her and she was very understanding. I also called the head of HR. Those people down there ...." His voice tailed off. "The long and the short of it is, you are our selection. Congratulations! You still want it?"

"Hooper," I said. "Not only yes, but hell yes!"

Home run!

21

THE BUTTERFLY EFFECT

Red Cross Disaster Relief vehicle in an undisclosed location

The "Butterfly Effect" is an observation of the real world. It's taken from chaos theory, which says that some highly dynamic systems, like weather patterns, are essentially unpredictable in the long term because the outcome of a complex event is so dependent on miniscule changes in the starting condition. This is likened to a butterfly flapping its wings in California that might cause a drought in the farmland of Nebraska.[5]

---

[5]   For more information on the Butterfly Effect find a book about Edward Norton Lorenz, one of the early developers of chaos theory.

Well, somewhere in North Africa, a flock of butterflies must have been flapping their wings like crazy, because on August 5, 2005, a tropical wave out of Africa joined forces with a group of previously unorganized clouds and became "Tropical Depression-12-2005." That undistinguished group of clouds organized itself like a spiral-shaped army column and went on to become a killer storm that claimed 1,833 American lives and cost the United States a record $125 billion dollars in damages. Its name, selected from an alphabetical list created long ago for these types of storms, was Katrina.

Karen and I watched the evening news regularly in 2005, and each night my trepidation grew and grew. It was as if I were watching that second airplane again on 9/11, coming out of nowhere and devastating whatever was in its way. I had grown up in Houston on the Texas Gulf Coast, and I knew very well the devastation that hurricanes could bring. I had witnessed many named storms in my own youth.

Hurricane Carla in September 1961 destroyed Galveston and to this day was one of the most intense storms to ever make landfall in the United States. My family drove 45 minutes to Galveston the next morning and spent the day doing whatever we could. By modern standards, she was not very deadly, with only 43 people killed, but I was never the same after I had witnessed the aftermath of that storm on Galveston Island. I was eight years old.

As we watched Katrina march across the Caribbean and into the Gulf of Mexico, Karen and I knew we wanted to do something. I talked with Karen about my idea and she agreed. As it happened, our timing was good. I had just been selected to move down to Washington and I could take leave, in the interim, to go down to Texas in the time between departing the FSDO in Portland, Maine, and arriving at the FSDO in Washington, DC, where I was about to start as the MAXJet lead.

Karen was available for similar reasons, leaving her job as an oncology nurse in Maine and needing to find a new, similar job in Virginia. She, too, would be in between jobs. I called the Red Cross chapter in Portland, Maine and told them we wanted to go to Texas to help out.

The Red Cross volunteer I spoke to said, "Well, we have some classes that you have to take first and then we can get you on our list."

"How many classes, and how long will it take?" I asked.

"Oh, you know the regular stuff. Sheltering, Feeding, Food Distribution, Warehousing, First Aid, Leadership in a Disaster Area. There's just a lot you need to know. We don't have many people going through these classes these days. It's harder and harder to find volunteers. Since you need all six classes, it's going to take a while to spool up all that you need any time soon. Maybe a couple of months."

"Okay. Not the best news I've heard all day but sign up my wife Karen and me. We would like to travel as a team."

"Okay!" She was happy to have two volunteers. "Your class starts Monday at 6:00 p.m. See you there. And thanks!"

After I hung up, I called my two bosses at the FAA and told them what I was planning and how I wanted to use my own personal leave time for the trip. I had learned, earlier, that I could not get the FAA to sponsor me to take time away from work to act as a Red Cross emergency volunteer. Besides, that sort of rankled me. I wanted this to be on me, not someone else. My two FAA bosses could not have been any more supportive.

Karen and I went to the Red Cross in Portland for training every day for almost three weeks. In that time, Katrina had, indeed, made her landfall and the disaster that followed required an "all hands on deck" approach. It was not difficult for us, really. It was simply just a matter of scheduling.

Karen, unfortunately, got a very disappointing piece of news. In a disaster area like the one at Katrina, volunteers and clients alike need to be able to eat what is available without regard to any food allergies that might incapacitate them. Karen has Celiac Disease. The news she could not go and help those people upset her. However, she did plenty to make it possible for me to go. She sold our house in Maine and did a million things to get us packed and ready for the move.

She followed my journey, and armed with what she had learned about the Red Cross and disaster response work, she was able to tell our friends and family all about what I was doing and why. Whenever they asked what they could do because she had inspired them so much with her messages, she could simply say "Contribute! Contribute to the Red Cross to help the relief efforts down there." Without her doing those things at home, I could not have made the trip at all.

I arrived in the disaster area on September 17th. Because it was late in the day, I was taken with about ten other volunteers to a shelter in Baton Rouge. We were all excited and could not get to sleep in the shelter that night. We were in a high school gymnasium that had two large floor fans to stir the hot, humid, hazy air. The triple threat from the Gulf Coast is "Hot, Hazy, and Humid." Those of us who had never done this Disaster Relief job before spent most of the evening trying to learn whatever we could from those who had.

The scene in the high school gymnasium

Here's the advice they gave us in the form of three critical "rules of thumb":

<u>Rule number one</u>: Everything takes longer in a disaster area. Traffic, lunch, calling home, everything. Count on it. Factor in twice the time it would take you at home and then add some more. Do that, and do not lose your cool.

<u>Rule number two</u>: Attitude is everything. Wake up every morning with two smiles: One for yourself and one for everybody else. They will appreciate it and you will be looked to as someone who is there to help. This will benefit you as well by removing unnecessary stress from others who have every reason to be stressed themselves.

<u>Rule number three</u>: Watch out for each other. Disaster areas are dangerous places with a multitude of ways to get hurt. Do not do anything stupid, watch out for each other, and you will be fine.

Every morning thereafter, I woke up, smiled my biggest smile, and walked around the area filled with other volunteers saying things like "Well, Hello, Sunshine," or "Good Morning! It's just another wonderful day in the disaster area," or even "Wow! You really killed the beauty sleep last night. Are you a model?" Or I'd make some other equally vapid comments.

I did this because the response was astounding. They did not know my background. I was a blank slate to them. All that they knew of me, was that I was the guy who always said something to make them feel good. And it really worked! I had fun with everybody there, even as they might be "having it out" with seemingly everybody else.

The first morning, we left the gymnasium, sleepy, and went down to the Disaster Headquarters. These are the temporary facilities where all the disaster response is coordinated. Everything the Red Cross can do is coordinated from this place, which is usually in an old, blown out Wal-Mart or Kmart or some other large place where the different disciplines could perform their jobs and also coordinate with other job functions by simply walking across the room.

Early on in a disaster like Katrina, there might be 600-900 people in that one room. From supervisors to volunteers and everything in between, everyone in the disaster response had to go there first. The noise was deafening.

Disaster Headquarters for Hurricane Katrina

It reminded me of the Big Green Machine in the Air Force. Not an exact comparison, but it was here that volunteers came to be sorted, issued orders, given whatever tools they might need, and provided transportation. Some got to drive, some did not. Some worked in roles they had worked before. Some, like me, were picked from an alphabetized list of names and told where they were going and what they would do once they arrived. Some might go to Mississippi. Some others might go to Texas. Some might have to wait until the next day for an assignment.

It was chaotic. These were people from all walks of life: truck drivers, school teachers, plumbers, pilots, doctors, and lawyers. They were people from every vein, but they had something in common – they asked for this job. Some sought a leadership position because many of them did not know how to lead people and they wanted to try. For a whole host of reasons, chaos ensued. Detail and perfection are the enemies of good enough and some of these people could get into the most unproductive arguments I have ever seen. I personally found that the less time I spent at HQ, the better. Once a volunteer learned the ropes of Headquarters, however, they could pull a string here and there with acquaintances from prior disasters, get the assignment they want, and be out of there.

I received an assignment to "Feeding," which initially disappointed me. I wanted to be out and about, not stuck in a kitchen cooking. But I was here to help, so I bucked myself up and got in the line. I was put in a van with six other volunteers and taken to Covington, Louisiana. We were assigned to the Spirit of America Kitchen.

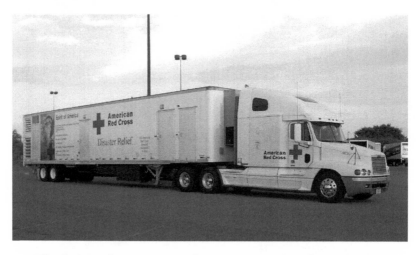

The Spirit of America Kitchen – Donated to the Red Cross by families of the victims of United Flight 93 on 9/11.

Much like any profession, I had to learn a new language when learning a new job. A good case in point is understanding the functions within a large semi-tractor-trailer truck converted to a mobile kitchen. The Spirit of America is a special truck, indeed. It's able to arrive anywhere in the continental United States in less than 48 hours and, within minutes can start churning out 20,000 hot meals per day to disaster victims. But there's a lot more than just this massive truck that's required. All the bulk food and refrigerator trucks full of ice and other food, the pallets of drinking water, the servers on site, and the drivers and crew on the Emergency Response Vehicles (ERVs) are all parts of the kitchen.

When I first arrived in Covington, I was asked if I had ever driven a forklift. Within ten minutes of my answering "no," I was stacking pallets of water here and there under the close tutelage of the man who taught this skill to most of the Home Depot forklift drivers in Louisiana.

Here I am in the driver's seat of a forklift and
a Red Cross Emergency Response Vehicle

My ultimate opportunity came when my supervisor asked me to drive an ERV, the Red Cross Emergency Response Vehicle. It's a big truck that looks like an ambulance and seems to be omnipresent in a disaster area. With this vehicle, volunteers can provide hot meals through the window (on the right side). They can also haul all kinds of cargo, like clean-up supplies, or surplus Meals Ready to Eat (MREs) from the military. They can also reach out to isolated areas and pockets of survivors who may not get rescued for days. One of the most important ERV roles is acting as the eyes and ears of the Red Cross decision makers.

"What did you see? How many? Where did you see them? Did they look desperate? Are they in need? Of what? Can we get it to them?" These were the questions we were asked every time we returned from our daily outings.

I was given a crew, I was given a mission, and I was given a vehicle to go out and do the mission. I arrived into a disaster area as a simple volunteer and I ended up as a crew commander. I do not know how it happened, but there I was, right in my own wheelhouse. I loved it.

Not to be denied, another powerful storm was raging in the Gulf of Mexico as we were doing our work on the north side of Lake Pontchartrain. It was Hurricane Rita.

We sat through Hurricane Rita's winds and rain as she made her landfall on September 24. Fortunately for us, she struck land on the other side of Louisiana, 300 miles to our west. On the day after her landfall, as she continued her trip north, we rolled up our sleeping bags and traveled west to the area she had touched the day before.

On October 1, my crew and I, like most of the other ERVs, were tasked to go out to specific areas and assess the need for the Red Cross's services. My crew and I came to a road that was covered by downed power lines, so I stopped. We could see a little town about a mile up the road but my map told me the road I was on was the only way in or out of the town. Being curious, I asked the crew to stay with the ERV and I began to walk. I had not gone very far when a rancher sauntered over to his fence.

"Howdy. You looking for something?"

I showed him my identification as a Red Cross Disaster Relief Service Associate, and he seemed unimpressed.

"Well, sir," I began in my best Texas drawl, "I am from the American Red Cross, and ...."

"We don't take too kindly to government people comin' around here tryin' to give stuff away. It always seems to cost us more in the long run," he said flatly.

"Sir," I pleaded. "The food in my truck is donated by people just like you or your neighbors. The meat probably came from cattle just like yours over there. The Red Cross does not get the bulk of their money from the government, at all. It comes mostly from your neighbors and mine. We're people who have watched this on our TVs at home and just wanted to do something, anything to help out but couldn't actually be here, like my wife at home in Maine. She's a nurse. She belongs here, but right now, she can't be here. So, they send us a few bucks and here we are with a truck full of hot meals. Do you want some food?"

"No," he beckoned up to a ranch house that must have cost millions. "We're fine here, but down in town ...."

"Do you know another way in?" I asked. "Red Cross has very specific rules about endangering my truck or my crew. I'm afraid I can't drive across those power lines."

He looked at me as if making a judgment on my character. "Maybe."

As the saying goes, "I'd rather be lucky than good." I was in the center of that little town in less than five minutes with a truck full of hot meals and the ranher was driving back to his millioin-dollar ranch..My crew went up and down in the small village explaining who we were and why we were there.

Soon, our truck became the center of all activity in the town. This is the perfect setcup for a Red Cross ERV in a disaster area. As the people gathered around our truck, they talked about the storm. They traded information about who needed help in the short term. We learned how many people we needed to feed and when they needed their meals. It was not only an opportunity to feed a town twice a day, we were also learning so much about the sorts of things we could do to help. And the people of this small town were forming bonds with each other that I knew were going to last for generations.

We continued our mission of feeding that town 385 meals, twice a day, for close to a week. At that point, no other truck or power company vehicle had been into the town yet, and I was nearing the end of my three weeks in the disaster area.

I was out in front of the kitchen, cleaning the truck. A clean truck is necessary to serve food from that truck – this is a hard-and-fast rule. There are lots of Red Cross rules on that and one failure on an inspection by the leadership may result in the team lead going back to washing dishes. My crew was helping me out, too, because they were also motivated by the feeling that we were really helping that little town in western Louisiana. It was perfect, even as it was fleeting.

I heard a voice behind me.

"Hendrickson? Robert Hendrickson?"

I turned around.

"Yes sir. Another beautiful day in the disaster area! What can I do you out of?"

That was my version of start-the-day humor that I had become known for.

"Your ride to Baton Rouge is here. We will leave in 20 minutes. Do you need help packing?"

"What? I thought I had one more day! The people in town are expecting me there in two hours and that is with one hour's drive time. I don't have time for this. I need to load up the ERV."

He then showed me that I was booked on a flight that evening and with the five-hour drive time to Baton Rouge, we were going to be pressed as it was to get to HQ in time to get me checked OUT of the disaster area and over to the airport in time. Time. Time. Time.

"Well who is going to ...."

My heart sank as I saw another volunteer walk up to my ERV ... MY ERV ... with a set of keys in his hand.

I told the driver to wait just a moment while I briefed my replacement on how to get into the town, when he was supposed to be there, who he should ask about what, and a million other things. Most of all, I stressed that dependability was important with these people. My replacement needed to run his acceptance inspection on the ERV and get moving in the next 30 minutes or he would be late.

As we drove out of the small kitchen, about one hour later, I saw him lazily starting the checklist which would take another hour, at least. I was angry, but I felt helpless. Our minivan made the journey to Headquarters in the expected five and a half hours, arriving there just after 3:30 p.m.

I entered the HQ and it was a lot quieter than it had been three weeks prior. I checked everything on my out-processing list: finance, health, transportation, that kind of thing. When I came to the last item, I questioned why I had to do it. Psychological assessment. Me? Why?

"Hi, Bob," the counselor began. "My name is Carl. How are you today?"

What happened next came as a complete surprise to me. Not to Carl, though. He has seen it a million times, I suppose. I began to cry. I cried. I sobbed. I told him about the millions of huge trees that were scattered around neighborhoods like a giant game of Pick-Up-Stix. I shouted. I cursed that stupid volunteer who stood up my town. I rose the roof, pounded on the table, and expressed three weeks of misery and frustration right there. The seemingly endless line of clients who came to the window of my truck and flatly said, "Yeah, we lost everything." The little girl in the white rubber boots that made her look so small. The houses that were simply gone. I cried and cursed and kicked until, eventually, I ran down and sat staring at a reflection of myself in a full-length mirror on the far wall. Carl asked me if that was all. It was, I assured him.

I was shocked at my behavior. I had never before expressed so much emotion in such a short time. My three-week tour of duty was up and I had to go home. I was drained as I was driven to the airport and flown home by the nice people of the airline.

Disaster Relief work is like a drug and it is very addictive. The user will experience higher highs, and lower lows without any intake of pharmaceuticals. If the user fails to find a way to let these emotions out in an appropriate way, they can be fatal.

Over the years, I helped out with Katrina (and Rita), Ike, Sandy, and Harvey. I would have done more, but I could not generate the required personal leave quickly enough to go as often as I wished. Harvey was my last trip because the symptoms of Parkinson's Disease made trips into disaster areas untenable for me.

Downed power lines block the way into this small town.

A hurricane in winter, Sandy, and I am in West Virginia!

22

JACKSON HOLE

Airbus A-320 airliner similar to the incident aircraft

I officially became an Investigator in Charge (IIC) within the FAA Accident Investigation Division (AAI-100) on January 20, 2008. Before I assumed my new duties, I traveled down to the FAA Academy in Oklahoma City for some advanced accident investigation training. When I returned from training, I was – on paper – an accident investigator.

AAI-100 had some interesting office procedures specifically designed to facilitate communications between investigators. All of us sat in cubicles arranged as closely to each other as possible. We knew that other FAA employees wanted the window seats in the largest offices. The IICs were different. We all wanted to be as close to each other as possible because it promoted sharing. Whenever I had a question, I could simply state my question over the cubicle wall.

"Hey, does anybody know if the nose wheel on a Grumman Tiger is castered?" Or, "What's the FAR (Federal Aviation Regulation) about requirements for recurrent training?"

If all my colleagues happened to be in on that day, I had five possibilities for a quick answer. Whenever they wanted to know about a heavy jet like a Boeing 747, they could count on an answer from me.

Every morning at 8:30, all of us in AAI-100 walked down the hall to the conference room and we hosted the most important meeting of the day: Round-up. One of the IICs or a Team Lead would host the meeting and the first thing he or she did, was to read through "the stack." The stack consisted of all the accidents, incidents, and occurrences that had happened since the day before in the United States. We also covered large, colorful, and interesting events from overseas. This review would take about 45 minutes on most weekdays to two hours on the return from weekends.

The variety of events touched on during this briefing was astounding. Everything from animal strikes on landing to light aircraft hanging from trees. Sadly, two or three fatal accidents occurred on a normal day. Many people around the HQ building would drop by to listen to the investigators educate the group on some point. When they had all the information they needed, they might wander off or stay a little longer. Round-up could be 30 minutes, or it might last all morning and into the afternoon.

Round-up served the purpose of keeping all of the investigators up to date on current events in everything aviation. What most people never saw because they were wandering in and out of the meeting, though, was how the investigators were listening quietly and filing everything away in their gray matter. Things would move along smoothly until suddenly an investigator would perk up with something like:

"Dave, about that runway excursion, did you say that that it was another normal approach followed by a floated landing by the copilot?"

Dave would thumb through the documents.

"Uh, yeah, T.R. Here it is. Yep, Southwest Airlines in LaGuardia. Looks like he went off the end."

"You remember the MD-80 from American I worked last month? Same kind of thing. Copilot flew a great approach, then floated the landing and never got it stopped."

Dave then might say, "I had one of those, too! A United 737 at Houston Hobby."

I would have to put in my two cents, of course. "There do seem to have been a lot of these lately. Maybe we have a trend here."

Hooper, our boss, would chime in. "Okay. We are getting into the winter months here. Last year was not good and this year is not looking good already. Let's emphasize this, folks."

Dave piped up. "What do we call it? Stupid Copilot Tricks (SCT)?"

We all laughed ....

When we were done with our little attempt at humor, Hooper got us back on course. "All right, let's track this under 'Runway Excursions.'"

There is simply no machine developed by man that is better at pattern recognition than the human brain. This is just one example of the unusual methods AAI-100 used to identify trends in accident data for years. It worked very well.

There was one rule of Round-up that was sacrosanct, however, and it was this: What was said in Round-Up, stayed in Round-up. First of all, the investigators had the absolute need to speak openly. We dealt with all sorts of people, from billion-dollar corporations to dirt farmers who happened to own a Cessna. We all needed to have the freedom to toss ideas around freely without any fear someone might be offended. This freedom to speak without filters was one of our big secrets in AAI-100, but only in Round-up.

Accident investigators also needed to feel free to vent their emotions in their own way, and this was the place. It was therapeutic and necessary for individuals who dealt so closely with death every day to get their feelings off their chests. Often, this was accomplished by some very irreverent comments that would be seen as completely inappropriate in another setting. Round-up was the place where we could wonder at the actions of a pilot who had killed himself by being, well, stupid. We could get it off our chests and move on. If a person from another office simply walked into Round-up and heard us laughing at something so inappropriate, they either needed to understand that this sort of banter was necessary for our sanity, or they could leave. It was as simple as that.

The date was February 25, 2008 – a little over a month since I began as an IIC. I had not left the office yet, because I was still learning. I was pretty new to accident investigation, so whenever any of the more senior investigators sat around the bullpen sharing war-stories about the accident investigations they had done and how they had solved various problems along the way, I sat and soaked it up like I did as a boy at the feet of MY three-wise-men (my father, my grandfather, and my uncle).

My mentor in the office was Tony James. Tony was a legend at AAI-100. It seemed that everybody in the headquarters building in Washington knew Tony. He was gregarious, and he had a southern accent that made him sound a bit like Andy Griffith's portrayal of the Sheriff of Mayberry (Andy Taylor) in his old TV show. Like Sheriff Taylor, many people thought Tony was a rube because he did not fit their image of what a smart man sounded like, but they liked him, nonetheless.

Those people could not have been more wrong about Tony. When it came to accident investigation, or anything involving aviation, Tony was always quick with an answer. More importantly, upon checking, he was always right. Tony was as sharp and on point as any investigator anywhere, and I was blessed to be learning from the best. It was easy for people to underestimate Tony and sometimes, that was his great advantage. I watched him and learned that the "aw, shucks" attitude often worked where other approaches failed. His casual, friendly approach disarmed people.

However, I was greatly humbled to know that he came to respect me, as well.

That day in February, Tony James was talking about what it was like on 9-11, as he was the only investigator (from any agency) to go to all three crash sites. Commander Bob (I became Captain Bob, later, in addition to Doctor Bob and Bob-the-builder – we had a lot of Bobs) was talking about nearly getting in a fist fight at another accident. Eric was telling us about his investigation of the crash of JFK Junior, and Christine was talking about an MD-80 at St. Louis that ran over a small airplane on takeoff. I did not have any stories to add, so I listened and learned.

We walked out of the FAA Building about 5:30 that evening. I hopped in my car and started my three-hour commute home. I had just walked in my front door and I had almost made it across the room to hug Karen when the phone rang. It was the Director of AAI-100, Hooper Harris.

"Hello Bob."

"Hi, Hooper, what's up?

"An Airbus A-320 with 125 people onboard just ran off the runway in Jackson Hole, Wyoming. I want you to be a part of the investigation team. Tony will be going with you since this will be your first with AAI."

"On my way," I said.

I finished walking across the room, hugged Karen, said good-bye, and I was gone to see the elk, the buffalos and this semi-crashed Airbus in Jackson Hole, Wyoming. The fact that nobody was hurt was a great bonus.

Tony was waiting for me at Dulles Airport, as he lived only about 15-25 minutes away. I showed up about 12 minutes before departure so we both made the last American Airlines flight to Jackson Hole with little time to spare. When we landed, it was just after midnight. I had requested permission from the crew to observe our approach and landing from the cockpit, so I could become more aware of the current flight environment at Jackson Hole. After that, I knew much more about the conditions faced by the crew of the A-320 that had suffered the incident earlier that day. I was amazed we could go from home to being at the scene of an accident halfway across the country so quickly.

During our flight, I logged onto the FAA's website and chatted with the FAA Command Post, and with Hooper, too. I learned that the weather was cold, but no precipitation was present at the time. Damage to the airplane had been superficial and they re-confirmed that nobody was hurt! Investigators love that call: "Nobody hurt."

Hooper went on to tell me that the airplane had landed normally and suddenly veered to the right, plowing directly into a six-foot snowbank that stopped it with just a bit of damage. The passengers simply exited the aircraft however they could and walked away into the freezing night. The passengers were all eventually accounted for. This took a while because some of them had walked to the parking lot after exiting the plane and driven home.

As we walked down the steps from our American Airlines 757, we looked across the tarmac, and there she sat: The A-320 that had gone off the runway. She had been towed into a normal parking space on the ramp and she looked surprisingly good.

"Tony," I said, looking at the A-320 parked 100 feet away. "Let's go do a walk-around." A "walk-around" is a cursory inspection of the aircraft from its exterior.

At this point I should mention that Accident Investigators have a special access card (it's referred to as "the magic identification card.") It allows us to go anywhere, anytime, without restriction at an accident site. The cockpit: yes. The control tower: absolutely. Go walk around a parked airplane surrounded by security: no problem. And so we did.

As we walked up to the nose wheel, we both noted extensive sheet metal damage caused by the snowbank that had stopped the runaway airplane.

I noticed there were lights and ports that were going to need replacement. I also was shivering. It was 6 degrees below zero. That's when I saw it.

The inboard (right) tire on the left strut was a flat! The outboard (left) tire on the same strut was fine.

The inboard tire was flat,
but the outboard tire looked brand new

"Tony!" I exclaimed. "I've seen this before! When I was working at the Washington Fight Standards District Office one of the guys brought me a picture because they couldn't figure it out and they thought maybe I could."

"Well?" Tony asked. "Did you?"

"Of course!" I laughed. "Piece of cake."

He grunted. "This little North Carolina boy is freezing. You can tell me all about it on the way to the hotel."

The next morning, we rode back to the Jackson Hole Airport across the cold but striking valley, taking in the Tetons in all their beauty. When we arrived at the airport at the designated time, we went into the airport's conference room and met the other investigators.

The team included representatives from every government agency, airline company, and aircraft equipment manufacturer that had a stake in the outcome of the investigation:

1. National Transportation Safety Board (NTSB) Investigator In Charge (IIC), Clint Jones (not his real name). The NTSB IIC was the head of the team.

2. FAA IIC (Tony James)

3. FAA assistant IIC (Me)

4. Four or five NTSB engineers

5. Five representatives from Airbus

6. Five from the Airline Company

7. Two from the pilot's union

8. Two from the engine manufacturer

9. Three from Bendix (the brake manufacturer)

10. Two from Goodyear (the tire manufacturer)

11. Five from the Jackson Hole Airport.

12. One Air Traffic Controller

As these things go, 38 people seemed a lot for a no-injury, off the runway jaunt through the infield. It was clear to all, though, that this event had the potential to have been catastrophic, so all of the entities involved sent small but significant numbers of investigators.

The NTSB IIC took charge of the meeting and asked everyone to introduce themselves. We went around the room until we had each spoken. Then the NTSB IIC spent 10 or 15 minutes discussing the event and assigning the investigators to different initial tasks designed to elicit the volatile evidence first. When he was about to dismiss all the parties to go out and get to work, he asked, "Anybody got anything before we go?"

Tony quietly raised his hand.

"I think Bob may have something." Then Tony looked at me.

As 37 sets of eyes all turned to me, I blurted out my recommendation.

"I think we should check the anti-skid wiring in the left strut. It's reversed."

You could hear the snorts of laughter.

The Airbus team leader looked at me and said, "No, no, no, Bob. That is not possible. There is only one plug per side, and they cannot be confused!"

"Same style plug, though, right?" I asked.

"Well, yes, but in 24 years, I have never ...."

The gentlemen from Airbus were so sure they were right, however, that they immediately went out to pull the two transducers from the landing gear strut (also referred to as the truck) to prove me wrong. It seemed so simple to them ....

It was now 9:30 and the temperature had risen to 6 degrees above zero as I watched the work progress on the wheels. It only took a few minutes to find the problem, and a few more to confirm it. They did not need to say a word as their faces told me everything I needed to know. I felt a rush of satisfaction, not because I was proven correct, but because I knew how we could fix it.

I did not need to move a single step from my perch above them on the steps leading to the aircraft door. I dialed Hooper on my cellphone.

"Hooper, it's Bob."

"Hi, Bob. We're still in Round-up. I'll put you on speaker."

"Okay, Bob. On speaker now. How is your first investigation going?

"Well, Hooper. I don't know. I think I've already pissed off Airbus and the NTSB."

I went on to explain the situation to the people at Round-up. I especially wanted Hooper to know. He was a great boss and supported us all the way.

I told them that when the pilot was planning his landing at Jackson Hole, he reminded himself and his crew that, first of all, it was going to be dark. Second, he saw there were forecast snow flurries. They weren't projected to be bad, but at 6 below, cleaning any accumulation off the runway might cause problems. At that time, the runway was clear of snow and ice, and his information said that it would remain so, but braking action might be a problem.

So, the pilot chose, very prudently, to land close to the approach end of the runway. This would give him the most possible remaining runway to get the airplane stopped as soon as they could *before* they entered the area at the end of the runway that was always more slippery.

He planned and executed the landing well, and he wound up in a snowbank anyway, wondering how he had gotten there.

Here is what happened. When the pilot hit the brakes on the short runway, he was doing something that pilots typically hate to do – he was being abrupt by stopping quickly. This rapid braking caused discomfort to his passengers. With the information he had, though, it was a reasonable choice.

However, this level of abrupt braking is rarely seen at major airports because they have long runways. Typically, the runways at places like LAX (Los Angeles), JFK (New York), MIA (Miami), or IAH (Houston) all have something in common. Their runways are anywhere from 10,000 feet to 13,000 feet long, plus they usually have an additional

1,000-foot safety overrun at either end. Those airports have one more thing in common: they are the places that airliners like the A-320 normally go. The runway at Jackson Hole (JAC), on the other hand, is 6,300 feet with no overrun. That's long enough for the Airbus A-320, but it leaves no room for error.

When the pilot aggressively applied the brakes, per plan, they malfunctioned. With the sensor lines swapped in the left truck, the central computer correctly noted that the inboard tire was beginning to skid, and so it sent a "Release" signal back to the place it thought it had come from. But with the lines swapped, the "Release" signal went to the wrong tire (the outboard one). Because it never released the pressure on the skidding tire, as it should have, that tire failed. The outboard tire, meanwhile, released completely resulting in no braking whatsoever from the left side of the airplane.

With one hundred percent of available braking action on the right truck (normal), and nothing at all coming from the left, the airplane veered right before anyone could stop it and everything was over very quickly.

'But that is not the worst of it, folks," I said to the people in Round-up. "The worst part is this. An airliner can fly around misconfigured like this for months and nobody will know, because they almost never use heavy braking at large airports. We do not know how many of these are out there, and they will not be revealed to us until the worst possible time, when the pilot really needs it."

This incident concerned me, because I had seen this situation before, as I had said to Tony. What I had not told him was that it was the same airline company. I was worried there might be other A-320s out there with the same problem waiting to bite them. There was only one way I could think of to find out.

After going through my line of reasoning based on my experience with this type of accident, I gave my recommendation to my boss.

"Hooper, I know it is getting late in DC right now, but I feel strongly that we need to run an emergency fleet campaign on all of this company's Airbus A-320s. Tonight." The maintenance test can be confusing, but if it is run correctly, it only takes a few minutes.

"That is going to piss them off," he said. "Anything else?"

"No, sir. That's it."

"What does Tony say?" Hooper asked. He wanted to be sure the experienced, old head investigator agreed with the new guy's recommendation.

"Hey, Hooper," Tony chimed in. "Bob nailed it. It's not a matter of if this happens again, it's only a matter of when. When these plugs are reversed, the resulting brake malfunction is bound to be dramatic. So, when it does happen again, it will probably be worse. We got lucky this time."

"Okay, let me set up a call. I'll get back to you in ten minutes."

After about 15 minutes, Hooper called again. He had the Principal Operations Inspector (POI) from the FAA Certificate Management Office (CMO), the Principal Maintenance Inspector (PMI) from the same CMO, and the Manager of the CMO, himself. These three people represented the FAA in essentially all dealings with the company, whose market-capitalization was over $10 billion.

As Hooper introduced the people on the phone to me, I began to see just how much influence I had in this new job. As my eyes grew wide, Tony smiled at me.

Hooper asked me to brief the accident. The three of them plus Hooper listened with great interest to my briefing, and after a few questions, they asked me, "What do you think we should we do?"

"Well, now that we know what the problem was, I don't see that we have any choice. We need to ground their entire fleet of A-320s and check them out without delay."

The PMI spoke up. "Man, they have over a hundred of them. Do you have any idea what that will cost?"

"Not as much as one airplane full of passengers," replied Tony.

There it was. All those millions of dollars in aircraft maintenance expenses based on the recommendation of one newly certified IIC from AAI.

If there was any power struggle at all, it was not even close. The FAA approved my recommendation immediately. The company did as they were directed by the FAA without complaint. Out of the hundred or so A-320s the company owned, they found <u>five</u> more planes that had this same problem and quickly corrected them.

That obviously concerned us. The next night, all A-320s in the U.S., regardless of company, had to perform the very same check. They found <u>six</u> more aircraft with brakes that were connected improperly.

I know this inspection also went worldwide, but I never heard the results. I understand that the corrective redesign of the brake connection cost Airbus a few million dollars, but that was infinitely better than a planeload of fatally injured passengers.

Determining the scope of the problem and directing the manufacturer to engineer a corrective solution was just the beginning. We needed to find out who reversed the wires and why they did it. Most importantly, we wanted to know how to prevent future occurrences.

The answer to many of these questions came later. It took only a few weeks to find the "who." There was a technician working at an independent airplane maintenance facility who was responsible. The technicians at this company were responsible for re-painting the landing strut to prevent rust – this was a normal preventive procedure. This involved a simple matter of just pulling the wiring while paint was being applied. The technician did not know that the two identical plugs were not intended to be used identically at all. The physical plugs looked identical, but they wore a paper tag with different numbers on the tags corresponding to where they should be connected. And to make things unnecessarily complicated, they weren't simple numbers like 1, 2, 3, 4. They were very confusing and there was no sequence to them at all..

I was happy and a bit proud of myself about the way this one turned out. Tony gave me the credit, although I learned some very important lessons at this investigation. They were life lessons that, only in retrospect, changed me as a person more than I knew at the time.

For instance, I learned that I had knowledge of things that others, often, did not have. To contribute to finding the solution, though, I needed to speak up. I had been in the right place to have seen this before. I was the only one of the investigators at Jackson Hole who had. If I had not spoken up when I did, the investigation would certainly have taken longer, and possibly even come to some tragic conclusions. I have a great deal of respect for the engineers at the NTSB, and other organizations, but if I can make their job easier, then we all can get to the fix sooner. I do not know if the days I saved by speaking up translated to lives saved, but it certainly did not hurt.

The second thing I learned was that I needed to temper my know-it-all attitude with some respect for the others around me. The aircraft accident investigators in my experience were the best and the brightest from their organizations. This is why they were chosen to be investigators from their organizations in the first place (the FAA and the NTSB included). I still had a lot to learn from them and I needed to maintain my credibility. I needed to recognize that and not disrespect the inputs of others. I saw how quickly a reputation traveled in this small community of aircraft accident investigators. By saying something inappropriate that might offend others, I might lose my credibility and fail to learn some critical thing from them that could help me later.

Abraham Lincoln once said, "It is better to keep your mouth shut and be thought a fool, than to open it and remove all doubt." But then, someone else also said, "If you see something, say something."

The fact that these two pieces of advice seem to be in direct conflict is an illusion that was finally revealed to me by this accident. In my new position, I was expected to speak up while maintaining my credibility. I had to do this while working with the smartest and best-trained experts that the aviation industry had to offer. The price of alienating the experts around me versus keeping my mouth shut was measured in human life. That is a sobering thought. People could die if I either failed to speak up or if I alienated the very experts I was working with. My epiphany came with the realization that we all faced the same problem.

This was the accident where I realized that I was one of them. I no longer felt like an outsider. That was a realization that moved me personally, and helped me save many lives through my contributions, large and small, to aviation safety.

In my life, those little steps I took that helped all of us move toward safer skies are the things of which I am most proud.

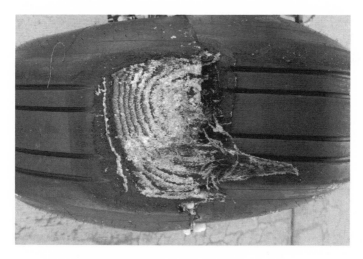

The flat tire from the Airbus A-320

23

THE ELEPHANT IN THE ROOM

The international symbol for Parkinson's Disease

How do you handle an Elephant in the Room? Introduce him!

For about a year, I had been settling into my job as an AAI-100 aircraft accident investigator. The job was exciting and challenging. I never knew from day-to-day where I would find myself in the next few hours. I could be called away anywhere from Patagonia to Peoria, or from Madrid to the Mojave Desert. I simply kept my "Go Bag" packed and handy so that I could go anywhere on the planet on a moment's notice.

We had jokingly suggested that the industry should schedule these things from 9 to 5 on a weekday, but it never seemed to work that way. It seemed that we were always the last to board our flight to *Wherever* and we always had a center seat in the back of the plane. Such are the penalties for showing up at the last minute and taking the last seat to *Wherever*. We never traveled in business class or first class. We always flew coach unless all the coach seats were sold out. Our second choice was the cockpit observer's seat (also known as "the jump seat"). Since I could bump anyone off the jump seat, I could always go on any flight I could physically catch.

Before anyone begins to salivate, he or she should know that the jump seat was designed by Vlad the Impaler. For example, in the KC-135, the jump seat was a milk stool with two of its legs bolted to the floor. In the Boeing 737 the occupant's leg room was about 4 inches, if the captain decided to cede it. The jump seat was not designed for comfort. It was put there for check airmen, such as me, to give check rides to flight personnel with a minimum of disruption to the cockpit routines.

Often, the jump seat was offered to us with a sly grin by the gate agent, thinking, I believe, that we would rather take the next flight. But whenever we were responding to an accident, time was critical. Evidence at the crash site was being trampled, rained on, pilfered, and otherwise destroyed every moment that we delayed.

My job was exciting, and I had enormous leeway from my Director, Hooper Harris, to do what I needed to do to get the job done. For example, most travel cards in the Department of Transportation (DOT) were limited to a couple of thousand dollars. This was plenty for most travelers going to a conference or something. Some of our itineraries, however, could easily run upwards of ten times that amount in addition to other expenses. Once, in San Francisco, I needed to capture a night video to "see what the pilot saw" on his approach to the airport (see Appendix 3). The only way to achieve this was to fly the very next night, keeping the airport lighting the same. The results were astounding.

I had to rent video equipment and guarantee the operating cost of a helicopter to fly us around to get those videos. Those two charges alone approached $30,000. Fortunately, even though it was a Saturday night, I had no problem because I was not the first to see the need for FAA IICs to be independent. Also, the California Highway Patrol stepped up and provided a helicopter, so most of the money did not need to be spent after all.

Our ability to go when and where we felt we were needed (anywhere in the world) and do whatever we needed to do without supervision was like having a length of rope. We could swing from it or we could hang from it. We kept this authority because we did not abuse it and because we produced results. And we still traveled coach.

One day, after having been an IIC for quite a while, I was walking down the hall of the 8th floor of the FAA Headquarters Building in Washington, DC, when I passed a friend and stopped to chat.

"Hi, Steve. What are you up to today?"

"Not much, Bob," Steve replied. "Say, did you hurt yourself?"

"No, I don't think so. Why?"

"Oh, I don't know. I saw you before. You were walking funny. That's all."

"Well, I can't account for it. I don't know what that's about."

As we went our separate ways, I did not think about it too much. I simply returned to my cubicle and went back to writing the IIC report I was working on that day. It was not until a couple of days later that it happened again. This time from someone else.

"Hey, Bob. How's it going? You know, you're walking funny. You okay?"

I still was not convinced, but by about the fifth time it happened I was starting to draw parallels to Rick Spott, my old friend from my Air Force days. He turned out to have ALS and suffered a very tragic, early death as a result.

The real clincher, however, was when Karen noticed something.

"Hey. What's wrong with you? You're walking like you've got a load in your pants. What's with that?"

I did not know!

Could I have ALS?

I made an appointment with a local neurologist; Karen went with me.

The date was March 12, 2008.

As we sat in the examination room, waiting for the doctor, I was nervous and Karen was looking pale. The only thing I could think of was ALS.

"Hello, Mr. Hendrickson. I am Dr. Jones. What brings you here today?"

I explained my friends calling me out for my supposedly "funny walk." I then asked him what he might be able to tell me about it.

I expected a long, drawn-out series of tests followed by days or weeks of confirming everything, but, instead, he said, "Do this."

He began rapidly tapping the pointer finger to the thumb on his right hand.

Always up for a challenge, I did the same.

"Now the left hand," he said.

I complied.

"Now, stomp your right foot on the floor as fast as you can."

He demonstrated and then I did the same thing.

"Now the left."

These exercises went on for less than three minutes. When he was satisfied, he sat down and looked me straight in the eye. Without preamble, he provided his diagnosis.

"You have Parkinson's."

Immediately, I asked, "Really? How do you know? What is the test? Isn't this a bit premature until the test results are back?"

He smiled and answered, "I just gave you the test. It's what we call a 'clinical diagnosis.' Other than the dexterity exercises you just performed for me, which were definitive in themselves, there are the other things."

"Yes?"

'I watched you as you walked in this morning. You are classic. The slow shuffle is standard for Parkinson's. Plus, there is your face."

"My face?"

"Sure. You have the flat expression which is also classic for Parkinson's. You think you are making expressions, but you aren't. When you think you are smiling, you aren't actually doing anything. 'Flat Affect' we call it."

He continued, "Oh, I have been doing this for twenty-eight years. You should get a second opinion, of course, but he's going to tell you the same thing I am telling you. You have Parkinson's."

"Wow," I said. "That's a relief."

His cheery expression faded, and he sat back down and looked at me.

"Son, do you understand what I am telling you?"

Now it was my turn, "Sure. You have given me a diagnosis of something I am going to have to live with, not something that will kill me next year. I would say that makes me a winner."

Well, sort of.

* * *

Only those people who have received a diagnosis like Parkinson's, understand what happens at the moment the Doctor says those three words: "You have Parkinson's." They can effectively hammer a stake in the ground to mark the huge left turn their life will take from that point forward. For the rest of their life, they will think about Parkinson's effect on them when they wake up in the morning, and it will occupy their last thoughts if and when they go to sleep at night. Every three to five minutes, they will do a self-assessment to see how they are doing. Are they going to fall down? Will the tremors cause them to spill their drink? How is their speech? Are they making any expressions with their face? How long since their last medication? How long until their next dose? Can they climb up those stairs or not? Damn, here comes the floor!

Their life has changed because they do not know how to do that much self-assessment and still hold other people in their thoughts, too. The Parkie, ("the person suffering from Parkinson's" becomes very wordy after a while) by necessity, becomes the most selfish and self-absorbed of people out there. At least, that is how their family begins to feel about their interactions with the Parkie. The truth is that no normal person could handle this full time for the rest of their lives, but every person who has Parkinson's is doing just that. Not by choice. They were not given a choice.

Inevitably, the symptoms will get worse. It is a progressive, degenerative disease, after all. Like the three rules of thermodynamics (restated): They cannot win. They cannot break-even. They cannot get out of the game.

My life changed on March 12, 2008. It is a date, among all others, that I will not, and cannot, ever forget.

When I returned to work the next Monday, I had to decide what to do about my diagnosis. Should I tell anyone? Should I tell no one? Should I tell everyone? This, I knew, would quickly become the "Elephant in the Room." Every time I walked funny, failed to smile at the right moments, or fell down because I was trying to get around without my walking stick, my colleagues would not know why. I owed it to them to introduce the Elephant and tell them how I was planning to handle him. Besides, the adage (about the Elephant) says to "introduce him."

* * *

And so, that is what I did. I explained to my colleagues that they might see me gone from my desk more because I was down at the gym or outside jogging around the Washington mall. I told them what to expect of me going forward, and how to know who I really was inside, not just what they saw. Finally, I reassured them that when I was no longer capable of doing a good job here, a new opening in AAI-100 would appear.

Their support was wonderful. They thanked me for letting them share my predicament with them. They saw that I never took advantage of my disease except to spend two hours a day at the gym. I was still traveling to twice as many accidents as some of my colleagues, and I carried my load, or more, without fail for 10 years.

I also investigated a lot of air accidents in that time. I assisted IIC Christine Soucy on Colgan 3407 which killed 50 people. I was the lead on the Air France 447 investigation, which was lost in the Atlantic Ocean and was not found for two years. I led the very first commercial space-fatal accident when the Virgin Galactic Spaceship 2 crashed during testing. I was the FAA's IIC for the investigation into the crash of a hot-air balloon in Texas that killed 16 people. I was the FAA's IIC investigating the fatal crash of a sight-seeing helicopter in the East River in New York, and many more. I investigated big crashes and little ones. All of us in AAI-100 did, but I finally got my wish.

Toward the end of my time at AAI-100, as I became one of the "Elder" investigators, I knew with absolute certainty that whenever there was a particularly difficult or technically challenging accident that had to be done correctly, my boss figured out some reason for the rotation to point to me, because I was one of his go-to-guys. He even told me once that I was his "fire-and-forget investigator." (Fire-and-forget is a reference to a type of air-to-air missile that requires nothing from its mother ship after it is launched on its mission). This was not to take anything away from the outstanding group of professionals in AAI-100, but it made me very satisfied to know that he felt that way about my contributions.

I am looking out over New York's East River during the investigation into the crash of a sightseeing helicopter which killed 5.

24

WHAT HAPPENS IN VAGUS

I was diagnosed with Parkinson's Disease (PD) on March 12, 2008. Technically, I suppose, I was diagnosed with Young Onset Parkinson's Disease (YOPD), as I was only 54 at the time. The difference is arbitrary, but the disease is the same.

My symptoms actually began before that date, but they were so slight that others had to tell me "you're waking funny" for me to realize that something was wrong. In retrospect, I know that I was experiencing symptoms even before that. I just never associated them with PD.

When I was still athletic and fully involved in sports and teams, I had no difficulties doing anything I needed to for my team. I could throw strikes from second base. I could throw a football a country mile – I had been born and raised a Texan and football was a religion there. I also ran track in my high school years. Even with a crashing hangover, I could run a 10.7-second 100 yard-dash.

Looking back, I can see there were some indications, but I did not pick them out at the time. One of the first things to go was my ability to throw a ball. It started slowly around 1980, when I was in my late 20s. I played some intramural baseball in the Air Force. I do not remember ever being a hero in the game, but I never really felt like a goat either. I was just an OK player. I liked to play second base because fielding was the important thing at that position, and I was pretty good with the glove.

Also, as a second baseman, the thinking of where I should be at any given moment was engaging and fun. Best of all, though, the throws I had to make weren't long. My throws would sometimes miss the target, occasionally even enough to pull the first baseman off the bag. But, instead of getting better with practice, I just kept getting worse. Whenever my stepson Kyle and I went out to the backyard to throw the baseball in the 1990s, my throws became downright embarrassing. I was able to hit everything in the yard, except his glove. I searched in vain for a reason. Was I just getting old? *Yeah, that's it,* I thought. *I'm getting old!*

Nope!

Down in the middle of the brain, at the top of the brain stem, is an area called the substantia nigra (which is Latin for "dark substance"). It is the place in the brain where almost all dopamine is produced. The neurons that make dopamine have so much melatonin they are permanently dark in color, which gives the area its name. Dopamine is responsible for many things neurological. It gives us feelings of pleasure, learning, motivation, kidney function, lactation, sleep, mood, attention, control of nausea, and pain processing, for example. The biggie for a lot of us, though, is movement. Dopamine touches almost every aspect of a person's existence as a functioning human being. When we run low on it, bad things happen to us.

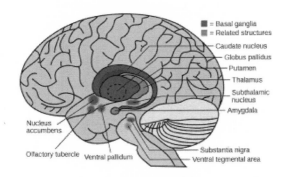

Cross-section of a brain showing substantia nigra and other important areas

I am often asked if this or that symptom could be from Parkinson's. My answer is always the same: "Is your symptom touched at all by the central nervous system? Then, yes. It very well could be, or not." Anything that interfaces with the central nervous system is suspect. Many diseases and dysfunctions, such as depression, bi-polar disorder, movement disorder, indigestion, vision problems, erectile dysfunction, and body temperature control are all touched by the central nervous system. The list is endless. It can be difficult to name anything that is <u>not</u> associated with the central nervous system.

This is why those of us who have Parkinson's (sometimes called "PDers" or "Parkies") are often called "snowflakes," too. This is not a reflection on our politics at all. The nickname refers to the observed fact that just as snowflakes are unique, Parkinson's affects each PDer uniquely. It can present itself anywhere, with almost any symptomology.

The typical way a neurologist diagnoses PD in the early stages is by observing a patient's body-movement coordination. Movement coordination is so easily affected that it stands out. This is why a PDer is easy to pick out of a crowd with their shuffling gait, their bent-over body, and their expressionless faces, quietly keeping their own counsel in the corner where they can be alone and relatively safe.

The PD symptoms that others cannot see are often worse. Indigestion, pain in the extremities, dizziness, loss of appetite, depression, and mania are, sadly, typical. Again, the list is endless.

In humans, the rule of thumb is that we can function quite well with only 20% of the neurons in the substantia nigra making their dopamine. This means that by the first time a person exhibits any symptom of Parkinson's Disease, more than 80% of the neurons in the substantia nigra are already dead and gone.

Traditionally, treatment for PD, and especially YOPD (as in my case), has been to slow the progression of the disease.

So, to help with this, the PD community has many support groups that encourage exercise, any exercise. There has been a great deal of progress in this area. PD sufferers, with their trademark shuffle, can be seen walking around the hospital grounds or the YMCA in little groups. It sometimes is surprising how many can be seen at the gym pumping weights, working up a sweat on the stair climber, or whatever suits them, then retrieving their walker or their cane and moving on to the next machine. It really does not matter *what* the exercise is, just as long as they do it regularly and vigorously.

Looking back, I can now see early signs of PD in my life. There might be a million reasons why I lost my ability to throw a ball way back when, but the idea that I might have the early signs of Parkinson's was not one of them in 1980-2008.

Oddly enough, I did not lose other abilities as quickly. I could still fly an airplane. I could even teach a student pilot how to perform receiver air refueling in a 500,000-pound KC-10, one of the most difficult maneuvers in aviation. Also, I could still drive a car, and engage in other activities that were highly technical or required great coordination. The truth is, I don't know why these areas weren't affected nearly as much, if at all.

Usually, I just had to try something and see what happened (in a safe way, of course). There were actually many areas in which my skills were less affected by the PD. I don't know if this was because these were *learned* skills as opposed to *automatic* skills like walking, sitting still, or keeping my balance. It seemed that my learned skills deteriorated more slowly. Eventually, however, the day came that I had to admit to myself and my supervisors that my ability to fly safely, like throwing the ball, were gone. That was very hard for me, and it contributed a great deal to my overall estrangement from others and my suppressed anger at the unfairness of it all.

The other thing I want to talk about is the origin of PD. What causes it and why are people so different in how they manifest symptoms? Nobody knows for certain. Most PD professionals feel there are two components that somehow join to make a person susceptible to PD. The first is DNA, those genetic aspects all of us are born with. There are researchers in labs all over the world trying to ferret out the gene, or the sets of genes, responsible for PD. There are no discoveries yet, but they are hopeful.

The second factor is thought to be some kind of environmental trigger. A concussion or other traumatic brain injury is one possible trigger. This "environmental" element can include exposure to chemicals, too. It might even be chronic fatigue, or loss of REM sleep over a long period.

The point is, even if a person has the genetic pre-disposition towards Parkinson's, then they still may not develop the disease unless there is a triggering event. Likewise, a person who suffers a brain trauma (for example), will not necessarily develop the disease unless they have the genetic pre-disposition. It takes both ....

The PD research effort in this area is also huge. Big money, and thousands of participants are heavily involved, including universities, hospitals, Michael J. Fox, and me. I participate in all the research protocols I can. As a result, I am routinely poked, prodded, asked to remember five colors, and count backwards by sevens. I have given blood and even spinal fluid to the cause. Honestly, I feel like a guinea pig and a pin cushion all rolled into one. I just want to send this disease straight to hell, where it came from and where it belongs.

Oops, a little of my emotion peeked through there.

PD people also have support groups like "Pedaling for Parkinson's." Dr. Jay Alberts, a Parkinson's researcher, discovered that when he put a PD sufferer on the back of his tandem bicycle, they were forced to follow along with his cadence on the pedals. Dr. Alberts is an avid cycler, so his cadence is about 80-90 rpm. That is quite fast, and most PD patients cannot keep it up for very long. But by putting them on the back of his bicycle, great results came to pass. He found that it was not the vigorous exercise that was important, but that the cadence had to be forced on the patient for a long period of time (typically 45 minutes or so). He claims miraculous results. Miracles do happen in little steps.

One of the techniques I learned in Air Force Survival School decades ago was to take my small victories when I can. One small victory of mine was when I rode the Register's Annual Great Bicycle Ride Across Iowa (RAGBRAI). I accomplished it twice. In 2010 it was just Karen, me, and 15,000 of our closest friends. The second time was in 2012 with Jay Alberts and his entourage, along with Karen, Lucas, and our lifelong friends, Rick and Martha Packard. It was fun while I could still do it. We raised awareness, money, and our spirits.

My 13-year-old son Lucas, me, Karen, Martha Packard, and Rick Packard dipping our tires in the Mississippi River to celebrate our successful rides in 2012

One of the clearest explanations of how insidious this disease can be to a PDer who is not yet aware of their affliction, is in the short, and easy read I have included in Appendix 1 (an article entitled "Loneliness, Social Isolation and Parkinson's Disease"). It is a fascinating look inside the Parkinson's sufferer that most would never know. I hope you will find as informative as I did.

The author focuses on the idea that neither the sufferer nor the ones close to them are to blame for the loneliness, social isolation, and other painful emotional consequences of Parkinson's Disease. This knowledge, sadly, is small comfort. It still hurts all of them, and the closer they are, the more it hurts.

One evening, in late 2020, Karen and I were having a lively discussion (a disagreement) about *how my Parkinson's was affecting our relationship* and there was a moment where we were both making our opposing points quite strongly. It was then I noticed something in her eyes I had never seen in 30 years of being married to her. I saw fear. Fear of me. I was crushed. How could she fear me? Of all the people on this planet, I would take a bullet for her. I have spent almost half of my life living beside her, raising kids, keeping (or helping to keep) the household, and never, ever raising a hand to her or any of the children. I rarely raise my voice. I was even diagnosed once as being non-confrontational. How could she be afraid of me?

In order to answer this question, I did what have always done. I hit the books. I did some research, and I learned the following.

One of the largest and most important nerves in a human's anatomy is the Vagus nerve. The Vagus nerve does not pass through the spine as most of the nerves associated with our motor functions do. The Vagus nerve is a cranial nerve, meaning it is right up front in our bodies. Among many things the Vagus nerve does, is being responsible for our facial expressions, our tone of voice, and all of the things we must do correctly to participate with other humans in a social world.

Evolution has hard-wired some very useful features into us. Karen has a healthy Vagus system, so she is adept at identifying when another person might be telling a lie, or is acting in a threatening manner. Sometimes, she does not even know when this is happening, because it is a reaction built in by evolution. It is as natural for anyone unaffected by PD as breathing. She is hard-wired to it and so are her reactions. This is where the famous "Fight or Flight" reaction comes from. Importantly, all of this happens in a normal human being without conscious thought. It is an instinct that has been developed over thousands of years of evolution. Asking her to turn it off is like asking her to stop feeling attracted to a baby. The problem is not that she is normal, the problem is that MY hard wiring has a short circuit, and I blame my Parkinson's for the loss of trust in my marriage. It is my fault, because I cannot control my Vagus nerve.

When I was flying for TWA, a flight attendant in training would ask the inevitable question: "How do I pick out the terrorist? What do I look for?"

The answer from the instructor was always, "Trust your gut instinct." And that works for a person who has a healthy Vagus nerve.

That is one of the main functions of a healthy Vagus nerve. It is so important to our social interactions that it is hard to overstate. I am the Parkie, the one who is broken. I am the one who is knowledgeable about the causes and symptoms of Parkinson's. And yet, I am powerless to stop whatever it is I am doing. I might get singled out as a terrorist if I am not careful.

Parkinson's Disease sucks in so many ways. The social estrangement of the Parkie is insidious and that can be deadly in itself, because of the resulting depression. All the dreams I once had for my own future had to be modified or abandoned. I can no longer say I am a pilot. I WAS a pilot. I am no longer looked to by anyone in my family as the person who can help them out of a jam. Now, they just look at me and wonder if I am going to hurt myself walking across the yard or if I am capable of driving the car to the store without mishap.

Right until the moment I was diagnosed, my loving and wonderful wife never had reason to doubt that I was there for her, no matter what. Now, it all has changed due to Parkinson's. I cannot blame her. Only someone who was super-human could possibly deal with all these fundamental changes in their spouse and not draw back. I am not super-human, and I fear she isn't either.

This is the predicament I find myself in with most of my friends with PD. For each of us, it is different, but for all of us, it is hard. For me, I can work through the Emergency Room visits to fix yet another broken bone. I can suffer through the indigestion. I can laugh at myself when I hit the rumble-strips one too many times on the drive to the doctor's office and Karen has to take the wheel. I can lay awake all night and I can fight my own desire to be someone that I am not anymore. I can type the same line five times because my fingers quit on me. In short, I can deal with PD when it comes to ME. What I cannot seem to change is PD's effect on my loved ones, and that makes me hate it like nothing else in my life.

I do have a lot of help, however, from my doctors and counselors. I am trying as hard as I can, and I have faith that a cure will get here in time to help me and all of my friends who have Parkinson's Disease.

Until then, I must isolate myself emotionally, if not physically. Whenever I reach out to my wife, the results are the same and I haven't found a way to tell her I am still in here, alone and unable to escape the prison that is Parkinson's.

25

ACCIDENTS THAT DID NOT HAPPEN

The Airbus A-320 missed the tail of the
Airbus A-340 by approximately twelve feet.

The First Officer, very busy keeping the instruments properly set and monitored, only had a quick moment to look up and see the view out the window. He saw something that worried him, and he expressed his concerns to the Captain.

"I don't feel good about this."

"Ask the tower if anyone is on runway 28R," the Captain responded.

After waiting a few moments for the frequency to be clear, the first Officer called the Air Traffic Control Tower and asked, "Tower, this is (xxxx). Just want to confirm, we see some lights on the runway in front of us. Are we cleared to land 28 Right?"

Unbeknownst to the crew, catching glimpses of something they did not like and prompting them to ask for clarification, the Tower could only see the construction zone on 28 Left from their vantage point. They were unable to see that the offending airplane was lined up to land on the crowded parallel taxiway, instead of the designated runway. The flight was set up for a fatal accident.

Aircraft accident investigators, on the whole, love a challenge. My 13 years in FAA accident investigation gave me many challenges and presented me with many victims. It is the victims who wear on an investigator, especially when the investigator is new to the job. It's easy to imagine that accident investigators prefer airplane crashes that have no victims. The only thing better than an accident with no injuries is an accident that did NOT happen at all. But how do we know that an accident about to happen was only averted at the last minute by a heroic pilot?

I am thinking of my KC-135 flight at Bergstrom, AFB and my aircraft commander, Rick Packard. He got a burning airplane back on the ground safely, under conditions that have been mishandled by many others. When an emergency happens like what we faced, where everyone can see what occurred and everything we did, and it will be subject to Monday-morning quarterbacks all over the world, it's easy to say that a potential disaster was averted.

Of course, there's the famous example of US Airways Flight 1549 Captain "Sully" Sullenberger, who ditched his Airbus A-320 with 155 people onboard in the Hudson River in 2009. Everyone survived, there were thousands of witnesses, and it was clear he averted a disaster through his skill and courage. There are certainly lots of examples of hero pilots, like Sully, saving the day. These are "feel-good" stories we all need to share now and then.

There are at least as many stories about pilots who came up short and died in a crash with all their passengers. For example, there's the tragic case of Air France 447, where everyone onboard was killed over the Atlantic one night. That investigation (one in which I participated, incidentally) took many years and millions of dollars to figure out what happened. The results of the investigation pointed to lack of experience on the part of the two First Officers who were on the flight deck while the Captain was getting some rest in the cabin (this procedure was perfectly normal).

Then there was the time a FedEx MD-11 was landing at Narita airport in Japan, when the copilot, operating the controls, lost control of the huge airplane and crashed on the runway. He killed himself and the Captain, the only two onboard that morning (this was also my investigation).

Sadly, it is all too easy to populate a list with names of pilots who died in airplane accidents. When we hear of a "save," we investigators like that a lot. Even if it is not a pilot who does the saving, we think that is okay, too. A higher power must have intervened in those cases, because, sometimes, there can be no other explanation.

What I described at the beginning of this chapter happened on July 7, 2017. An Airbus A-320 was approaching San Francisco International Airport (SFO) just before midnight. The flight was just a little late, which usually isn't a big deal. In this case, though, the flight was late enough to make a big difference. The pilot's dispatch paperwork (his flight information) included all of the news for SFO they needed. There is a large section of the paperwork that contains Notices to Airmen (NOTAMS). These NOTAMS are the legal notification of the most current information for every pilot to fly to and land at airports throughout the world. It included information on SFO, for instance.

The pilots studied their NOTAMS that night based on the planned time of their arrival in SFO. There was not much of consequence. The winds were predicted to favor Runway 28, which consisted of two parallel runways, designated 28 Left and 28 Right. However, after 11:00 p.m., there was a huge change. Runway 28 Left was scheduled to be closed for maintenance. That would not have been a problem for these pilots, except they were two hours late getting started. They just missed the fact that the NOTAM about the runway closure now applied to them.

The delay meant they would also be fatigued at the time of their arrival in SFO because they would be arriving around midnight (which, importantly, was about 3:00 a.m. for their "local body time"). Finally, Air Traffic Control cleared them to fly an approach unique to SFO that involved the pilot picking up the landing runway visually.

Accident Investigators sometimes focus on the most innocuous events and our leadership can be counted on to point out the waste in government dollars that represents. We almost did not investigate this event, because it just did not seem to be a big deal at first glance. The airline crew went around, nobody was hurt, and they landed normally on their next attempt. As it turned out, I am glad we did launch on this one, because it turned out to be huge. The airplane on the approach lined up to land on a taxiway that was parallel to Runway 28R. Again, no harm no foul, except that the taxiway had some airplanes waiting to take off.

The investigators were able to establish that the pilot of the approaching airplane was easily drawn into the error he made in lining up on the wrong runway, and that the other airplanes he almost hit were invisible to him until the very last possible moment. People with the benefit of 20-20 hindsight did not understand how four airliners could possibly be invisible from his position until they saw the video that I and the NTSB IIC took the next night for ourselves.

"(xxxx), SFO Tower, you are cleared to land 28 Right. There's no one on 28 Right but you." The controller had picked up his binoculars and confirmed that 28R was clear and all the construction vehicles were on 28 Left, where they belonged.

Seven seconds later, everyone on the Tower frequency heard someone on the radio ask, "Where's this guy going?"

Four more seconds elapsed, and they heard, "He's on the taxiway!"

The approaching aircraft initiated his go around before the next call from the Tower. Researching this event, there are some sources that line up the times on the tapes vs. the video. This makes it appear that the offending aircraft did not go around until tower made the call, and that is a mistake. We knew then and we still know now that the Tower's call to go around came about two seconds too late.

The first Officer of the approaching airliner issued the "go around" command. He did not feel comfortable even though the ATC Tower told him that they were all alone out there. Though he could not recall any details, I believe that when the second airplane in the taxiway queue turned on his landing lights, he and the Captain both realized how badly they had misjudged their approach and landing. The first Officer said the magic words ("go around") at the same moment the Captain was planning to go around but just hadn't pulled the trigger. The Captain might have initiated the go-around in another second, but that would have been too late.

The first Officer was the hero on this flight because he said two words: "go around."

In addition to the 140 people on his A-320, the four airplanes on taxiway "C" were a Boeing 787, an Airbus A-340, another Boeing 787, and a Boeing 737. A total of well over 1,000 people in the cross hairs were spared that night by one person speaking up when nobody else did.

Their main gear came within six feet (officially) of the Philippine Airlines A-340 that was sitting number two in line. Six feet at a sink rate of 700 feet per minute (fpm) works out to roughly one-half of a second. One second more, and San Francisco would have made the 1977 Tenerife collision between two loaded Boeing 747s (an accident which cost 548 lives and is still the single deadliest airline accident ever) look small by comparison.

It really was that close! The story does not end there, though.

After the crew had barely averted disaster, they landed on their next approach normally and never said a word. The Captain claimed he did not know on that evening that he had come within six feet of disaster. This meant that the airplane was never taken out of service for our investigation. More critically, the cockpit voice recorder (CVR) entries were recorded over when the airplane flew back to their home of origin just a few hours later. By the time investigators became aware of the scope of the incident, the information from this flight had been overwritten.

When we investigators traveled to the pilots' home office a few months later, we were armed with a lot of answers but just a few questions. In the intervening time, armed with the tower tapes, witnesses, our own videos and the inflight data recorder, we learned just about all there was to know, except how and when the pilots had reached the very late decision that they should abort the landing and attempt a go-around. This gap in our knowledge was mostly because of the overwritten CVR.

There were five of us acting as investigators for this trip and we had practiced this briefing/presentation on our superiors and other interested parties before we traveled. We felt we were ready.

We sat down in a non-descript conference room with the two pilots, their union representatives, the Chief Pilot of the airline involved, and a full boat of human factors, specialists from the NTSB, FAA, and Airbus. We started by showing them pictures. We showed them maps. We showed them flight data. We showed them eyewitness reports. We explained how all that information fit together to build a very complete timeline of the event down to tenths of a second where appropriate. We talked for about two hours to them, explaining what we had learned about their event. We did not need to pile on when it came to telling them how many people were placed in danger. They had known that for quite some time because of media reports. To this point in the discussion, they had not seen the video. Every time we finished a section of the briefing, we returned the overhead projector to the photograph that is labeled "SFO Rwy 28 L/R." (Appendix 3)

We investigators had not even asked our first question. This was hardly the grilling that pilots are shown to get from the FAA and the NTSB as depicted in the movies!

After we set the groundwork, we asked everyone in the room if they were still questioning how the pilots could miss such a dramatic thing as four airliners sitting on the place where they intended to land. A few hands went up indicating their skepticism. We then pointed to the photo that was, once again front and center on the white screen. Then came the showstopper.

I asked everyone present in the room, "How many airplanes are in your sights in this photo? Remember, we took this shot the next night. The moon, the lighting and the visibility were as close to the same as humanly possible, but we did not speak to these airplanes to ask them to set their exterior lighting or how to point their airplanes on stopping. As far as they were concerned, this was just another night at San Francisco.

"The photo is taken on a one mile final, about 20-25 seconds from touchdown, or 10-15 seconds from contact with the second airplane waiting for takeoff.

"As you can see, the photo is taken from the vantage point of an airplane approaching Taxiway C in error. The runway over there on the left is actually Runway 28R, the intended landing target. So where is Runway 28L? The answer is, its lights are off so as to avoid confusion.

"Also remember this, you have all been sitting here in this very comfortable, quiet briefing room. You are well rested, and you have had this picture in your face for over two hours. It is not 3:00 a.m. and you are not doing anything but sitting there."

The silence in the room was thick. Nobody wanted to be the first to guess.

In fact, nobody ever did.

Here is the answer. In reality, there are only two airplanes in that picture. The Airbus A-340 is easily found because of his wingtip lights. The other aircraft was more difficult to see, but eventually, we did as we flew by in our helicopter. Coincidentally, it was another Airbus A-340. The pilot of that airplane had turned off his high intensity lights as a courtesy to the other airplanes in the area. Together, those two aircraft probably carried over 500 people.

By doing this, we made the point that fatigue, expectation bias, physical conditioning, flying at a high speed that does not leave much time to change a pilot's mind, as well as many other things, can easily lead to such an error. The people who raised their hand when I asked my earlier question in this room looked at the pilots differently after that.

Then, because the NTSB had not yet released the video of the low pass to the public, we asked everyone to leave the room except the investigators and the two pilots.

We ran the video, which is only about two minutes long and clearly shows the disaster that did NOT happen.

Then we returned the photo of the landing area to the screen and invited the others back into the room.

It was at this point that the first Officer needed a few moments. He was very pale. When he returned five minutes later, he looked at me and said, "I can't believe we came that close to all those other uh, uh, *planes.*" He looked sick and he had to leave again.

When he returned the second time, I took him aside and asked if he wanted to talk about it later. I gave him my card and invited him to call me if he ever had anything he wanted to talk out. We already had everything we needed, and the Captain was not particularly helpful at coming clean on who and how the go-around was called, but I knew who I believed.

That's okay. I think we did all right.

San Francisco Air Traffic Control decided that this close call was not to be ignored. Upon learning that 100% of all wrong runway landings were during a *visual* approach, they directed that there would be only instrument approaches to SFO after dark. Also, the FAA spent the next three years working with airports, software developers, and the Air Traffic Controllers Union developing and fielding a modification to an existing ground radar system already found at most major airports in the U.S. This system, now in operation, will sound a loud and persistent alarm in the control tower 15-30 seconds before any airplane on arrival lines up for landing on any surface other than the runway onto which they have been cleared to land.

My efforts centered on that radar modification and hoping these two pilots would tell other pilots about their experience. I'm sure there is no more believable person than a pilot telling a roomful of other pilots how he *almost* killed more than a thousand people.

In every case, there is no one-size-fits-all for corrective actions. Sometimes it might involve just talking to the pilot, whereas sometimes we may have to tell a hundred software developers, a thousand bureaucrats, and ten thousand union members what they need to accomplish, together. By contrast, it seems so easy to tell the CEO of a multi-billion-dollar corporation that he will need to ground his fleet of expensive airplanes until his company can fix them. I've done that, too.

The overarching guiding principle is always "Whatever it takes."

26

NO CALL

When I had told all my FAA and NTSB colleagues about my elephant-in-the-room in March 2008, I had also promised to retire before my disease became a problem for others in my office. In August 2017, I was feeling better than I had in a long time. But I had also just finished a particularly grisly accident investigation into a hot-air sight-seeing balloon that hit power lines and crashed in a fireball that took the lives of all 16 people aboard. They never even had a chance to run. The crash site was horrific. The pilot on this flight was a very personable and friendly entertainer of the passengers. He also happened to have more pharmaceuticals (mostly illegal) in his body than any of us investigators had ever seen anywhere.

I was having a difficult time controlling my body temperature during this investigation (a common symptom of

PD). It was hot. The temperature in Lockhart, Texas hovered between 98-106 degrees F and the humidity was visible in the air. The combination of heat and humidity was one of the factors in the balloon crash because it severely limited the pilot's ability to see the power lines.

I was only 63 years old and I found myself in the air-conditioned command trailer more often than I liked. I just could not move in the heat. This was in spite of the fact that for the last 10-plus years, I had been exercising at least three times per week, spending hours in gyms and outside on the Washington Mall running, and I am *from* Texas. I hated to admit this to myself, but I was not progressing. The Parkinson's was taking over.

I was able to hold the disease at bay for a little while, but PD was bigger and stronger than I was. That was why, on my birthday in 2017, I announced to everybody in the office that I would retire on my 65th birthday one year from then. I reasoned that this was the new retirement age for airline pilots, so if they could do it, I could, too. I saw this as good a time as any.

When I went to my financial advisor, he gave me some excellent news. He made matters very clear to me that now was the time. I had an okay nest egg and it turned out that money would not be a problem in my retirement.

I went home after that balloon accident and I made very sure that Karen understood the financial situation. We projected our future income with and without her needing to work until her own retirement date.

Karen, he explained to us, could improve our income for a few years but in the long run, her income would not make a very big difference in our bottom line if she were to wait for full retirement age. For her, that would be in May 2022.

Looking at a future of increasing disability, I wanted to do some traveling and camping throughout the U.S. while I could. I even had a bucket list of places I wanted to see and things I wanted to do. Karen, though, was understandably uncomfortable with leaving work earlier than she needed to and she resisted retiring early. This is just one example of how PD had a negative impact on our lives and our relationship, completely separate from the physical challenges involved.

On July 31, 2018, my telephone rang again, as it had many times before. An Embraer E-190 had failed to take off and had crashed beside the runway in Durango, Mexico. Fortunately for the lucky passengers, airplanes are built much stronger today than they used to be. No one in this crash was seriously injured even though the two pilots had attempted (on purpose, apparently) to take off into a thunderstorm and had encountered a microburst that caused the wings to lose lift and the airplane to come back down to the ground at about 170 miles per hour. It skidded off the runway and went through the weeds for about half a mile before coming to rest.

It was fairly easy to drop this one into the "stupid pilot tricks" column. Since it was not a U.S.-based company that was responsible, the American investigators came home after about three days. This was a quick-and-easy accident. There were no fatalities, no injuries, and we were all home within three days.

The Embraer E-190 that crashed beside the runway in
Durango, Mexico
There were no serious injuries

Under the rules of the duty roster in my office, because the trip was only three days, I had the choice to accept this as my international trip and go to the bottom of the list, or I could stay on top of the list and hope I could get one more trip. My retirement date from the FAA was looming on my September 29th – my 65th birthday.

I elected to launch once more before I retired.

After I returned from Durango, Mexico, I was using my spare time completing some IIC reports and finishing up my travel voucher for Mexico. In reality, I was waiting to launch to do just about anything. I was #1 on the international list and standing by to go.

On Sunday, September 9th I was at home when the phone rang.

"Hello Bob?" It was Jeff Guzzetti, the head of AAI-100. Jeff had come to us from the NTSB so he already had a number of accident investigations in his resume, including an Alaska Air MD-80 which lost control of its horizontal stabilizer and crashed in the Pacific Ocean, killing all aboard, just as the two pilots were talking live to Air Traffic control. Jeff had a reproduction of the offending jackscrew that caused the accident in his office as a reminder. Because he supported us so completely, and had a great knowledge of accident investigation, we IICs were very happy about Jeff coming in to be our leader.

"Hey, Bob, I am just calling around to get a snapshot of everyone's availability for a launch on Monday. Some of the guys are gone to conferences. We may need to ask you to cover for a 20-fatality accident in the Sudan. Are you available?"

"Of course, Jeff! Send me in! I'm always ready!"

"Okay, Bob," Jeff chuckled because this was always my standard answer. "I have you down as a definite 'maybe.' Gotta go, that's Command Post on the other line. I'll call later."

I went to my car and retrieved my Go-Bag. I had first packed an overnight bag in my car while I was a pilot in the Air Force. Since then, the contents of that bag had been upgraded significantly. With all the equipment I now had, I could almost pretend that I was in my own office from anywhere. I could connect to all of the internet sites I needed even when I was standing in the middle of a farmer's field in Nebraska, and I had a week's worth of clothes. I pulled out my parka and my long gloves and my mukluks from the bag. I didn't think I would need those in September in Sudan. I did, however, put in a water purifier just in case, and returned the bag to my car.

I awoke Monday morning at 3:30 a.m., my normal time, and looked for any messages. None. I was not surprised by that because I knew they would let me sleep if their attempt to get any flights to Northeast Africa were successful.

I did not find anything in my messages for me, but I did find that I was copied on a back channel message that said AAI would be launching that day for the LET-410 in Africa. Why had Jeff not called? I checked the launch list and noted that my name was still at the top of the list, but no call.

So, I waited until 8:00 a.m., and I called him.

"Hey, Jeff," I said. "Are we going to launch on this LET-410? The death count is up to 20."

"Why, yes, Bob," came his quick reply. "I think we are sending David. He is over at the Sudanese Embassy, getting his visa right now and his flight leaves this evening."

"Oh. Okay," I said. "My name is still on top of the list if another one pops up."

"That's the thing, Bob. You have just about 20 days to retirement. I know that you have a lot of accident investigations on your desk. Between now and your retirement, you need to hand them all off to the other investigators."

"So, does that mean I am done? Should I unpack my Go-Bag?"

After a long pause, Jeff replied.

"I guess so."

"Okay then."

My Go-Bag was a Travel Pro roll-aboard suitcase. It went with me everywhere in addition to another normal suitcase for regular trips. The Go-Bag contained all of the tools of my trade, including a computer, two cell phones, and their chargers. It also contained enough clothing for me to get by for a short time. I carried medications and protein bars in there, too, just in case.

For me, my Go-Bag was a very powerful symbol of my identity. I had carried it for 40 years, because who I am, and what I have done in my life, is facilitated and symbolized by the things in that bag.

It did not take long to unpack my Go-Bag and put everything away, but the impact on me of doing so was profound. Unpacking my Go-Bag marked the end of 40 years of my life. Unpacking my Go-Bag was, strangely enough, one of the most emotional parts of my retirement from a very amazing career.

The old Travel Pro bag is sitting beside my desk even now. I never know when I might need it again.

27

THE FACES OF DBS

I retired from the FAA on September 30, 2018. The extra day beyond my birthday on the 29th was added to line me up with the end of a pay period, but it was a Saturday, so it really did not matter. My farewell party in DC was very nice and was attended by many of my colleagues. I got a plaque thanking me for my service with the FAA. I received my credentials ("Creds") in a picture frame. Some nice people from the tenth floor (the administrative offices where FAA leadership resided) came down to see this Hendrickson character they had heard about but had never seen. I had fun hanging out with my wife and kids in Washington, DC during the days leading up to the retirement, and just like all of my other adventures in my life, when it was over, it was over. End of story.

The retirement decision was not my choice. Parkinson's Disease had made the choice for me, but I was ready to move on. I have always had difficulty seeing my future with a dark cloud hanging over it and I was not going to let the PD define who I was or what I could do.

We all went home and immediately I realized that I did not want to be bored in retirement. It had been more than a year that I had been encouraging Karen to retire with me so we could see the world at ground level instead of at 39,000 feet, as I had already done so many times in my flying career.

At first, she claimed she wanted to make more money for our nest egg before she retired. Then there were a number of other reasons she did not wish to retire. It soon became clear I was powerless to persuade her. I was frustrated that I could not convince her to adventure with me.

I was stung by her refusal to go on an "extended vacation" with me. This was the sticking point between us that contributed to a lot of our problems later.

I admit I was being very selfish about what I wanted. I could see my Parkinson's getting worse despite my interventions, and that scared me. I was afraid I would be bedridden by the time she decided to quit working. That, in turn, made me angry because of what I perceived as the most egregious sin of all: wasting precious time. And in this case, it was my time we were wasting. I could not seem to make her see how important it was to me to have her with me as my traveling companion, wife, and lover. We were at an impasse.

For her part, Karen did not wish to retire. Her reasons are hers to know, and I never made a dent in her resolve. In fact, she dug her heels in even more. In frustration, because I felt my time was running out I raised the stakes by telling her, "I really want to go on this great RV adventure across the U.S. while I still can. If you won't come with me, then I will have to go it alone, because I do not know if I will be ABLE to by the time you make up your mind."

Karen is a very self-reliant, confident, and resourceful woman and my reaction to her continuing her work was not positive. Again, I felt I was facing a drastic change in the very fabric of my life, and the choices I faced were impossible. Do I stay in Maine and wait for an early death or hit the road and risk my marriage? I hated the dilemma I faced. Damned Parkinson's.

In the end, I went on my trip alone. My body was warm in South Texas, but my heart was cold. After six months, I came home to my wife. But Karen, it seemed, had been irrevocably hurt by my ultimatums. She didn't show it outwardly. She just looked through me as if I weren't there. Eventually, she did not even bother to do that. She began to project a lot of her anger onto me. This only made me feel more isolated and I did not know what to do about it.

We began a slow death spiral into our own personal hells. We went so far as sleeping at opposite ends of the house. Things were not looking good for the two of us.

At the same time, I was secretly paranoid about one thing. Every time I stumbled and every time I fell, I could see my mobility slipping away. Falling and injuries often mark the beginning of the end for older people. I know that mobility is the key to fighting PD. I was scared to think that one little injury would lead to another, and another, and eventually, after a year or two immobile in my bed, it would be bye, bye, Bob!

That was NOT what I wanted for my end-of-life story!

I gave in to the anger. I blamed Karen for all of this and drove the wedge even deeper between us. That was on me.

There was hope, however, in the form of a medical procedure called Deep Brain Stimulation (DBS). By 2020, DBS had been around for about ten years, but it was still considered very experimental, and the results were not consistent. By the time I felt I needed it, the procedure was becoming more and more commonplace.

DBS is a procedure offered to PD sufferers as a therapy that can be helpful with some of their symptoms. In my case, alleviating my walking difficulties was all I really wanted. Thankfully, I did not suffer from tremors.

DBS is performed in a hospital by a team of doctors. The team consisted of a wide variety of medical specialists, including a neurosurgeon, a Movement Disorders Specialist (MDS), and the "usual suspects" (anesthesiologists, special nurses, students, residents, representatives from Medtronics (the device manufacturer) and more people than I can name). At any given time, during my three trips to the Operating Room (OR), I could count 15 to 20 people in there. All of them were actively engaged in my operation. The operating procedure is very impressive, and it takes place in the hospital's "Big OR." It takes a neurosurgeon who thinks and acts as a "team player" to orchestrate this effort, because he is the leader of this group that is about to perform *elective* brain surgery on a human being!

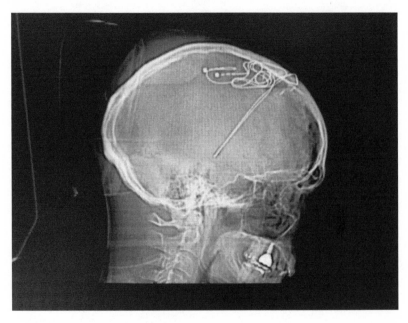

This is an x-ray of my head with the electrodes in place

The purpose of this procedure is for the team of doctors to place one (or two) electrodes directly into the patient's brain. This operation must be done with the patient wide awake and talking so they can direct the doctor to the right spot.

I was hesitant to go ahead with this surgery, even though my doctors recommended it. I couldn't believe that putting wires in my brain was not risky, despite what they said. I started and stopped on this once in October, 2019. Adding to my fears, Karen did not want me to do it. She thought it was too risky. For a while, I agreed with her, but eventually the potential rewards of the operation outweighed the risks. I arranged to have the three days of surgery in February, 2020.

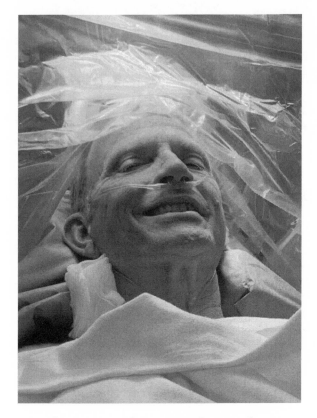

*This picture of me was taken at about
2.5 hours into the 3.5-hour DBS surgery*

I cannot begin to describe the sensation of having another person (the neurosurgeon) drilling two three-quarter-inch holes in my cranium and inserting wires deep into my head. The brain itself has no pain receptors, so it is not that pain is so difficult to endure. It's the cumulative fatigue and the insults to your body that are so wearing. It took me months to completely recover from this operation. I am told I'm fortunate that my operation went comparatively well.

Some of the aspects of the procedure were fascinating, even as I was enduring the surgery. For example, there was a specialist at my side we all called "the whisperer." For this procedure, he is the one person in the room who is entrusted with telling the neurosurgeon when he has found the most optimal placement for the electrode. This process may take hours because the site they are looking for is about the size of a Tylenol and is located deep within the brain. The whisperer, however, watches squiggles on a TV and listens to the noise in the patient's brain. Eventually, if all goes as planned, the whisperer nods to the neurosurgeon, turns and walks away.

Recovery from DBS surgery is long, and the results are not guaranteed. Close to 25% of patients will have an infection in the implant area as a result of the procedure. If that happens, the team must go in again and remove everything they did before. After six months to a year, they decide if they want to do it all over again.

I have now seen a few of the other patients who have undergone this procedure, and their faces tell a story, that I can only point to and say, "Look at that!"

Their faces are shown in Appendix 2 "The Faces of DBS." They are a testament to the strength, resilience, and attitudes of those who would choose such a path. I could not be prouder to call them my friends. These Parkies are mentally strong, and they have gambled on an experimental medical procedure that will define the rest of their lives, for better or for worse, or maybe even result in their death.

I hope that by looking at them, the reader will have an appreciation for how strong these people are. I believe this inner strength shows through in their faces. They are fully into life, and they refuse to let PD rule them. In short, they are the most inspirational people I know.

28

EQUAL TO THE LOVE YOU MAKE

Now, in November, 2020, I am still retired and exercising whenever I can. I am doing much better regarding the PD now that my Movement Disorders Specialist (MDS) has adjusted my DBS settings a few times. The DBS is unbelievable in so many ways. When the doctor adjusts the voltage and I suddenly stop shaking and I can walk again, that sense of safety is hard to overstate. My self-confidence is back, and I can do normal activities with much less medication and far fewer side effects.

Karen still works at the hospital from 8:00 a.m. until about 9:00 p.m. Her job as a nurse makes terrible demands on her for very little pay, but I am so proud of her and her commitment to the health of her patients that I cannot find the words.

I still love her and forgive her. I hope she finds forgiveness in her heart for this old Parkie. I want her back and I will keep my heart open for her until that day. She is the love of my life and I will be hers whenever and wherever she wants me.

I have a pretty good track record for getting what I want. I know that it entails making myself right for the job and not just running in and pushing other people around. I am confident that I can do what it takes. I have plenty of motivation and with DBS, I feel I now have plenty of time.

As for Karen, Maine is her home. Her family is here. She wants her end-of-life story to originate from right here. I am okay with that so long as I can travel down to warmer temps during the cold months in the Northeast. I feel drawn to where I grew up in Texas, in particular. We can see where life takes me during those times when I'm away. I have all the time in the world.

Bob Hendrickson. Last Seen in Rockport, Texas

29

SO WHAT?

I am proud and feel very fortunate that I have done many things in my life that were exciting, challenging, risky, and downright amazing. I have been dealt some bad hands in my life, but I have had great adventures, too. I would not trade my life for anyone else's I know. I haven't collected a lot of money, but I have had enough. I have had what my fellow international pilots, after an ocean crossing, would call "a good run."

I have had my share of sorrow and grief and more than my share of amazement at the wonderful place we all share here on Earth. I have flown across the great oceans, I have taught others how to do so, and I have picked up the pieces of the unlucky few who did not make it. But through all of that, I have tried to learn from their mistakes and communicate my knowledge to others so that they need not make the same ones.

I only hope that the world is a little better place because I was here.

I feel it's time to get in my camper and go to South Texas for a while.

In a lot of ways, it's not nearly the challenge of going to the Moon that I had set out for myself in 1974, but I hear they are building rocket ships to Mars down in Boca Chica. I think they just might need someone who can do what I can do!

Hmmmm … **Mars!** *I'll bet I could do that! All I need to start, is a plan!*

Bob and Karen

APPENDIX 1

THE VAGUS NERVE AND PARKINSON'S

Author's note: Very few people understand why it is that people suffering from Parkinson's Disease (Parkies) act so strangely. In addition to the tremors and lack of coordination in their physical movements, their behavior is, well, weird! Perhaps this article will explain the case better than I can.

LONELINESS, SOCIAL ISOLATION, ESTRANGEMENT AND PARKINSON'S DISEASE April 25, 2018
Re-Printed with permission of the author.
Outthinkingparkinsons.com © Dr. Gary Sharpe

"The single biggest predictor of rate of Parkinson's progression is if you answer true to 'are you lonely'?"

This finding by Dr Laurie Mischley, who monitors the progress of symptoms of more than 1,500 people with Parkinson's Disease, is perhaps one the most tragic aspects of the disease in our modern society, in which we people with PD may find ourselves heading toward this outcome by default. Indeed, I have lost count of the number of people with PD who have said something to me along the lines of "my friends and family have abandoned me/don't visit/lost touch". The negative feedback loops between loneliness and disease progression can be one of the most vicious circles of PD. I speak from personal experience also, because at my lowest point, I too had become very isolated, virtually alone in the house and barely going out.

This issue runs much deeper than simply being due to people in pain naturally pushing others away and wanting be alone, or otherwise healthy people naturally feeling uncomfortable or awkward around someone who is chronically ill. To understand the deeper root causes of estrangement and isolation in Parkinson's Disease, we need to first understand some background about the biological evolution and neuroanatomy of the human nervous system.

- The vagus is a cranial nerve that emerges from the brainstem

- We have twelve cranial nerves, and some of them control the muscles of the face.

- Cranial nerves are not equivalent to the nerves emerging from the spine that control the skeletal muscles of the limbs.

- Facial expressiveness, the middle ear, the neck and the voice are regulated by cranial nerves emerging from the brain, distinct from the spinal cord regulation of the limbs and torso.

- The vagus nerve, however, is involved not only with the regulation of facial muscles, but also the cardiac and pulmonary muscles - heart and lungs.

- The vagus nerve therefore is a two-way communication channel connecting the face to the organs, and the body to the brain.

- It allows brain function to affect the visceral organs and vice versa.

- It links the regulation of the heart to that of the facial muscles.

- Enables our inner physiological state to be written our faces and to be heard in our voice.

- Enables changes in our facial expression or tone of voice to affect heart/breathing rate.

- Many health problems are known to include *both* poor regulation of the heart and dampening of facial expressiveness, vocal range, auditory hypersensitivities, and stiff neck.

- These health problems are connected with loss of ability of the vagus to regulate the muscles which it supplies.

- This heart-face integrated system comprises an evolutionary purposeful "social engagement" system, allowing humans (and other mammals) to work together in social groupings.

- This social engagement is downregulated/inhibited in those conditions which include expressionless faces, auditory and language, and neck/shoulder problems as symptoms.

- A damped social engagement system is bilaterally associated with increased fight-flight or freezing behaviors.

- When this system is damped early in life, it can lead to significant developmental problems.

The above is tremendously important for people affected by Parkinson's Disease to understand in terms of their own health, since PD is a condition so highly associated with a blank or expressionless face, weakened vocal abilities both in terms of volume and emotional content, lack of ability to move head, and issues with listening. Indeed, these are all classic symptoms of PD, which get worse as the disease progresses.

However, even more important is in understanding the resulting impacts of these features of the disease on other people and hence on social interactivity, due to the profound implications for social isolation, Again, the following is adapted from Dr Stephen Porges' works on the polyvagal nervous system.

- Neuroception is a process by which our nervous system evaluates risk without requiring conscious awareness nor cognitive evaluation.

- Automatic programs involving parts of the brain which are constantly checking for cues of safety, danger or threat.

- These processes can then shift our internal physiological or emotional states according to the real time outcomes of their evaluation.

- Although we may not even be aware of specific cues which cause a particular change in state, we may be aware of the resulting shifts in internal state, e.g.

changing heart rate, gut feelings or sensations, an intuition.

- Our evolutionary survival actually depends more on these visceral instincts which reside in the structures of our nervous system, than on our cognitive or conscious self-awareness

- The evaluations however are highly individual, and that which some people's system detects as safe and comfortable, others detect as risky and frightening.

- People with faulty neuroception detect threat/danger when there is none or feel safe when danger is actually present.

- This component in our nervous system, which is meant to be self-protective, also allows us to evaluate the states and feelings of other people.

- Through neuroception, our bodily functions act like a lie detector, which is not always correct.

- We are highly tuned to the physiology and intentions of others through their facial expression, vocal tones and volume, gestures and posture, and how these, in turn unconsciously make us feel.

- When neuroception detects safety in another person, it can also trigger internal physiological changes, such as hormonal ones, which translate to trust, social interaction and relationship building.

- Different physiological or emotional states can therefore be identified with optimal social behaviour or efficient, adaptable defensive states, or dysfunctions of these.

- From this perspective many health issues and diseases can actually be understood as problems with neuroception and atypical behaviours from nervous system [dys] regulation resulting in difficulties turning off defensive strategies ["stress"] or disabling spontaneous, normal social interactions to occur.

- Challenges current social and healthcare models, such as schools, hospitals, institutions, as these may be inadvertently set up to trigger unconscious feelings of danger and threat especially in sensitive, traumatized or unwell people, e.g. low frequency background noises, types of lighting, demeanours, attitudes and atmospheres.

- However, also points to new strategies based on "neural exercises" which regulate faulty neuroception, such as the "Integrated Listening System", or the neuroplastic techniques covered in Dr Norman Doidge's book "The Brain's Way of Healing".

We currently do not account at all for how these social engagement and neuroception aspects of our neuroanatomy affect the real life experiences of people with Parkinson's Disease. This is unfortunate, since to re-iterate, the social engagement functions are significantly downregulated in people with PD through atrophy/inhibition of the cranial nerves (both sensory and motor): facial expression, volume and emotion in voice, light in the eyes, natural movements of the head, ability to listen, all become dulled/inhibited/ absent as the disease progresses. The important point to stress is this lack of social information and of the normal social signals emanating from people with PD will trigger unconscious and automatic responses in other humans. Indeed, the facial and vocal "masking" in people with PD will tend to set off the neuroception in others, creating sensations of un safety in their nervous system, simply because the person with PD isn't giving out the "normal" social or externalized cues that their biology expects. This results in a "threat" type response in other people via the hardwired nature of the evolutionary biology of their neuroanatomy. It is extremely important to stress this is *not* about other people doing anything wrong or being to blame or even conscious of this, it is about unconscious automatic response hard wired into the human nervous system, for extremely good evolutionary reasons for our own survival.

Conversely, inhibition of the social engagement nervous system, due to atrophy of cranial nerve function, means people with PD also often can't read the social engagement cues of others correctly. This, in turn, may result in inappropriate interruption of normal social interactions or the misreading of the physiological or emotional states of other people. Again, it is to be stressed that this is not done on purpose, and is without attached blame, usually occurring without the person with PD even being conscious of it. This unconscious breakdown in normal social graces and responses can also lead to estrangement and further social isolation. Porges even has a term for this: "biological rudeness", which he defines as *"a cascade which starts with a lack of reciprocity to a spontaneous social engagement that triggers an automatic state of defence and ends with an emotional response of being offended that may lead to an aggressive reaction."*

A very clear demonstration of this reflexive aspect of the human nervous system is given by the famous "Still Face" experiment with infants.

It is my hope that through having increased awareness of our own biological reactions, we can all begin to understand the challenges that people with conditions like Parkinson's Disease face in social interactions every day. Again, people with PD may have combinations of all these features present a lot of the time, including unreadable faces, reduced voice content, and lack of animation.

In pointing people to their own inherent visceral reactions to these types of symptoms, I hope we, as a society, can acquire an increased understanding and, more importantly, increased compassion, towards people with Parkinson's.

Disease as they attempt to manoeuvre through a very difficult terrain of social interactions, which is currently strongly stacked against them.

APPENDIX 2

THE FACES OF DBS

In the pages that follow, I present very little in the way of explanation. These are some of my friends who I have come to know because of my battle with Parkinson's Disease and because I have had the Direct Brain Stimulation (DBS) surgery, myself. To put it bluntly, this is elective brain surgery. It takes a special kind of person to choose this path. These faces convey an inner strength that defies words. I am proud to present the faces of these fighters here.

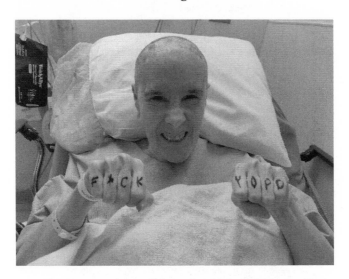

This Page: I love this Lady! So inspirational!

*(F*CK YOPD is a reference to
Young Onset Parkinson's Diseaase.)*

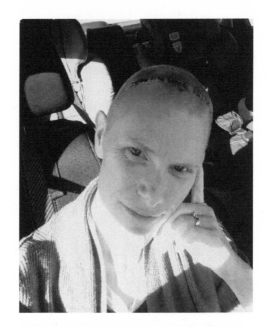

This is Redbadger Queen

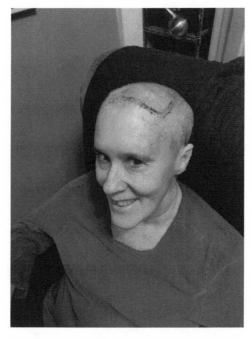

Stephanie is a mother of two children.

This is Melissa the day she was discharged

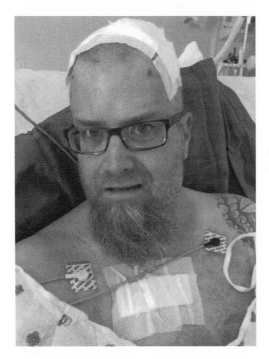

This is Darryn, March 3, 2019 – I thought I was smiling! LOL

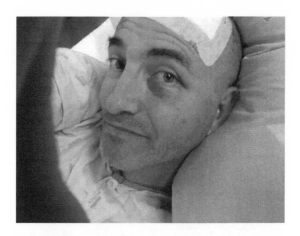

This is Andy. DBS Surgery in 2014.

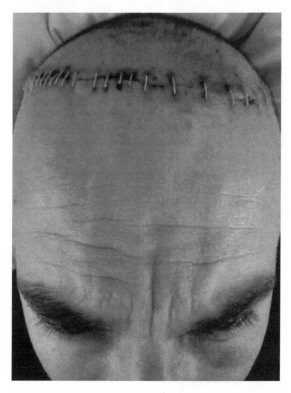

Here is Andy. "New wiring installed, (Yep, those are staples.)
Nothing turned on (yet), still wondering if it's all going to be
worth it?"

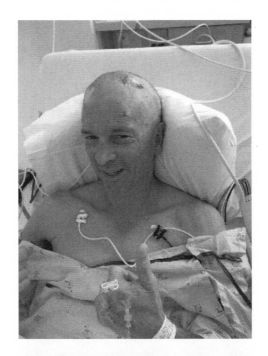

This is Christian Edison

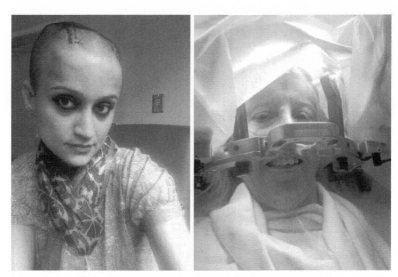

On the Left: Still very attractive with the seams in her head.

On the Right: John. Some Neurosurgeons like the stability of the "Halo."

This is Sara and her dog . . . Spot?

Lisa

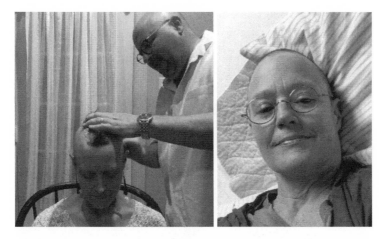

On the Left: Shaving me the night before...a little Mohawk! Lol

*On the Right: I was on an antibiotic drip for
2 months 2 times a day.*

My husband had to give it to me.

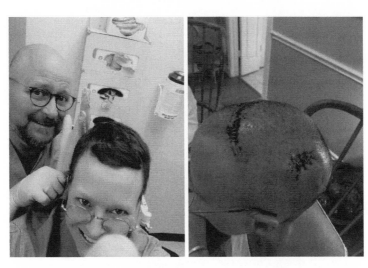

*On the Left: My husband and I getting
some tests done before my DBS.*

*On the Right: I went home and you could tell,
the infection was in the back of my head.*

Lisa

There is the face of a fighter!

APPENDIX 3

SFO RWY 28R

In chapter 25, I tell the story of an accident that did not happen. In the narrative, I refer to this photograph. It is reproduced here so that the reader may appreciate the problems that it reveals.

A photograph taken of Runway 28 Right (RWY 28R) at
San Francisco International Airport taken
24 hours after the approaching A-320 went around.

Made in the USA
Middletown, DE
29 January 2023

23210031R00172